H. P. Lovecraft in the Merrimack Valley

H. P. Lovecraft and Charles W. Smith, Haverhill, October 1931.

H. P. Lovecraft in the Merrimack Valley

David Goudsward

Hippocampus Press

New York

Published by Hippocampus Press
P.O. Box 641, New York, NY 10156.
http://www.hippocampuspress.com

Cover photograph © 2013 by Logan Seale. It depicts the B&M
Railroad bridge crossing the Merrimack River into downtown Haverhill.
Constructed in 1919, it was Lovecraft's first sight of Haverhill on most
of his trips.

Cover design by Barbara Briggs Silbert. Hippocampus Press logo
designed by Anastasia Damianakos.

First Edition
1 3 5 7 9 8 6 4 2

ISBN 978-1-61498-057-5

CONTENTS

This book is dedicated to the last of the great Haverhill historians.

Gregory H. Laing
(1947–2008)

If you would understand anything, observe its beginning and its development.

—Aristotle

FOREWORD

Kenneth W. Faig, Jr.

One of my hopes is that we will eventually see a reference work on the life of H. P. Lovecraft as comprehensive as William E. Baringer's *Lincoln Day by Day: A Chronology 1809–1865* (Morningside, 1991). The very considerable archive of surviving Lovecraft correspondence should facilitate the chronicling of the author's life—where he was, whom he met, whom he wrote to, what else he was doing day-by-day in as much detail as can be reconstructed from the surviving record. We already have landmark books like *An H. P. Lovecraft Encyclopedia* (Greenwood Press, 2001; rev. Hippocampus Press, 2004) by S. T. Joshi and David E. Schultz, and Joshi's own monumental *I Am Providence: The Life and Times of H. P. Lovecraft* (Hippocampus Press, 2010), but I am convinced that a day-by-day chronology would provide opportunities for new research. By the 1930s it is probably a rare day that we can say nothing about what H. P. Lovecraft was doing. In the 1920s, however, I suspect that there are still weeks for which we cannot account for his activities. The lacunae for prior decades must be even larger, although researchers like Chris Perridas have gradually been ferreting out information, even for the early decades when there was little to distinguish H. P. Lovecraft from the rest of humanity.

Now comes forward David Goudsward, native of Haverhill, Massachusetts, author, family historian, and librarian by profession, to illumine for us one fascinating aspect of H. P. Lovecraft's life which has been explored only lightly in the past—his association with the Merrimack Valley and fellow amateur journalists Charles W. "Tryout" Smith (1852–1948), Myrta Alice (Little) Davies (1888–1967), and Edgar J.

Davis (1908–1949), who lived there or nearby for most of their lives. What a trio—the elderly sage of 408 Groveland Street in Haverhill, old enough to be Lovecraft's father; well-traveled near contemporary of Lovecraft who may in fact have been a romantic interest—so much for the theory that Sonia Greene (1883–1972) and Winifred Virginia Jackson (1876–1959) were the sole combatants for Lovecraft's affections; and the last president (1925–26) of Lovecraft's beloved UAPA faction, who was in fact young enough to be Lovecraft's son.

Although he had an especial love for his own native Rhode Island—where Roger Williams had settled to find refuge from the Puritan theocracy in Massachusetts—Lovecraft also was very well read in the history and legendry of New England at large, and especially of Massachusetts. In his travels in Massachusetts, he found many inspirations for his remarkable fiction, and the Merrimack Valley contributed its own share. David Goudsward is the author of four books on New England antiquities: *America's Stonehenge: The Mystery Hill Story* (with Robert E. Stone; Branden Books, 2003), *Ancient Stone Sites of New England and the Debate Over Early European Exploration* (McFarland, 2006), *The Westford Knight and Henry Sinclair: Evidence of a 14th Century Scottish Voyage to North America* (McFarland, 2010), and *Dighton Rock and Miguel Corte Real: The Portuguese in 1511 Massachusetts* (McFarland, forthcoming). He also is an authority on horror fiction and film, having written four books in this domain with his brother Scott T. Goudsward. From his backgrounds as an historian of New England antiquities and as an authority on horror literature and film, Goudsward brings a rich frame of reference to his exploration of connections to Lovecraft's Merrimack Valley.

Goudsward is not the kind of family historian to be content with "genealogy lite" based on electronic searching of Ancestry.com and other family history resources. He is of the old school, known to visit city halls, county courthouses, deed registries, and other archival repositories in the pursuit of his research. In this remarkable extended treatment of Lovecraft and the Merrimack Valley, he brings to life not only the author himself, suddenly freed to broaden his life with travel after the death of his mother on May 24, 1921, but also his three

Merrimack Valley associates, whose lives had their own ups and downs, and the rich historic, architectural, and folkloric heritage of the Merrimack Valley that formed so vital a part of Lovecraft's touring. Goudsward, I think, makes an excellent case that Newburyport—beautifully restored in recent decades, but very much in decay when Lovecraft visited—formed an important part of the author's inspiration for his fictional Innsmouth. And he reminds us that Lovecraft visited the Merrimack Valley sites associated with the Quaker poet John Greenleaf Whittier (1807–1892), many of whose poems drew upon the lore and legendry of his native Merrimack Valley and New England more generally.

I hope that an in-depth consideration of the influence of Whittier's poetry on Lovecraft's works will be one of the results of Goudsward's thorough research of Merrimack Valley. A paper "Lovecraft and the Slums" would be yet another possible by-product of Goudsward's work. Broken-down survivals of ancient dwellings—and the secrets lurking within them—could form only objects of social concern for most contemporaries because of the misery of the inhabitants. Only a few photographs—emphasizing social and hygienic considerations—survive of yesterday's slum environments. Yet how much treasure the aficionado of Lovecraft's work might offer today for a comprehensive photographic record of the slums of Newburyport, Boston, and Providence as Lovecraft and his fellow explorers experienced them. I wish I could bring to bear Goudsward's skills as a family historian to research some of the Providence slum sites that inspired Lovecraft, such as the ancient house at 6 Olney Street on Stampers Hill (demolished in 1931 for the widening of North Main Street) that inspired the Joseph Curwen house in *The Case of Charles Dexter Ward*.

I invite the reader to sit back and enjoy a neglected slice of the life of H. P. Lovecraft. David Goudsward is a thorough guide and he will reward you both with succinct prose and with well-chosen illustrations. Knowing that you may well wish to experience some of the Merrimack Valley sights seen by Lovecraft, he provides a practical guide for doing so as well. His book *Ancient Stone Sites of New England* contains a similar appendix, with very practical advice. Goudsward's fellow New England researcher Robert Marten took me to see some of these sights when I visited him in the mid-1980s, but without a guide like *Ancient Stone Sites,* I am sure I would never have found many of the sites myself. One summer while I was a graduate student at Brown University in 1970–72, my parents came to visit, and I still remember the difficulty we had getting into and out of Marblehead, Massachusetts, by automobile. Surely it was worth the effort, but New England's rotaries, one-way streets, and unmarked routes make an experienced guide like Goudsward very valuable.

If every day of Lovecraft's life were as well-documented as the days in the Merrimack Valley that Goudsward narrates in the present volume, we would be well on the way to a completed *Lovecraft Day by Day.* The life and work of a genius like Lovecraft will continue to provide fascinating topics for research as the readers of the future encounter his work. David Goudsward opens up new pathways for understanding Lovecraft and his world in *H. P. Lovecraft in the Merrimack Valley.*

PREFACE

I doubt if any of the popular josses of the present will be heard of at all in fifty years. But I am willing to gamble that you and your work will be known: perhaps not to a very large audience, but certainly to a select and faithful one.

—Clark Ashton Smith, in a letter to H. P. Lovecraft, 1 March 1933

In the mid-1980s, I began a working relationship with America's Stonehenge, a.k.a. Mystery Hill in North Salem, New Hampshire. And although I have written books on that site and similar stone sites in New England, I've pondered one vexing question for decades for which I have no definite answer: Did literary horror legend Howard Phillips Lovecraft base his descriptions of the stone-strewn ruins and stone altar atop Sentinel Hill in "The Dunwich Horror" on a visit to North Salem?

Even after moving from Haverhill, first to Pennsylvania and finally Florida, I found myself returning to the question as new publications on Lovecraft offered new clues, or as some odd alignment of the constellations gave birth to a new idea pursuing possible leads. In all these cases, the path led to Haverhill Public Library and Greg Laing in the Special Collections room. He and I shared a special rapport—we both understood that local history was more than the published history—it was the quirks, scandals, and unwritten aspects of local history that made it come alive.

We also had an odd bond: my late mother-in-law Virginia Bilmazes Bernard had hired him back when she was director of the library. So every visit to Special Collections was a reunion—he would let me know what new tidbits had come to light about the descendants of

Haverhill's founding fathers, and I would dutifully report on what was new among my in-laws. On one such trip in 2002, Greg mentioned that yet another reference librarian had directed a Lovecraft fan to Special Collections in search of a specific landmark associated with Lovecraft's various visits to Haverhill. He knew I had researched Lovecraft's visit to Mystery Hill and suggested I could pull together my notes and produce some sort of booklet of local landmarks to which he could then refer "those Lovecraft people."

This project was Greg's idea, and his intuitive familiarity with Haverhill's history was the only reason it could be started at all. His untimely passing made it much more difficult to finish. I think it safe to say, in light of the fact that we were originally envisioning a 6- to 8-page booklet, we both underestimated the number of locations in the Merrimack Valley that merit mention.

While I hope local residents will enjoy the text, this book was written with the assumption that the reader is familiar with the works of H. P. Lovecraft but not with the Merrimack Valley. If you are unfamiliar with the works discussed, such as "The Dunwich Horror" or "The Shadow over Innsmouth," I suggest you proceed posthaste to the nearest public library or bookstore and discover the cosmic insignificance of mankind in the uncaring universe as envisioned by Lovecraft.

It will always be a great regret of mine that Greg Laing passed away before this project came to fruition and he will never be able to use it to gleefully send "those Lovecraft people" away from his realm.

—DAVID GOUDSWARD

Lake Worth, Florida

ACKNOWLEDGMENTS

Graham Blackhurst
Chief Richard C. Borden, Haverhill Fire Department
Marlene Boucher
Donald R. Burleson
Brien Corey
Sue Gagnon, Merrimac Public Library
Jessica Gill, Newburyport Archival Center
Scott T. Goudsward, New England Horror Writers
Hal Inglis, New Hampshire Society of Genealogists
S. T. Joshi
Diane Kachmar, Florida Atlantic University
Arie Koelewyn, National Amateur Press Association
Greg Laing, Haverhill Public Library
Donovan K. Loucks, The H. P. Lovecraft Archive
Suzy Martin, Hampstead Historical Society
Mary Ellen Moulton
Stan Oliner, National Amateur Press Association
W. H. Pugmire
Andrew E. Rothovius
Merrily Samuels, Hampstead Public Library
Louise Sandberg, Lawrence Public Library
David E. Schultz
Philip A. Shreffler
Robert E. Stone, America's Stonehenge
Kathleen Uman
Tim Weisburg, Spooky Southcoast

And special thanks to Chris Perridas and Kenneth W. Faig, Jr.

H. P. LOVECRAFT IN THE MERRIMACK VALLEY

408 Groveland, Haverhill—"Tryout" Smith's home from 1904 until his death.
Courtesy the Trustees of the Haverhill Public Library, Special Collections Department.

Chapter 1

TRANSFORMATIONS

In 1913, the letter column of the popular magazine *Argosy* published the comments of a reader criticizing the purple prose of author Fred Jackson. Jackson was a writer of unremarkable melodramatic romances, but he was popular among the readers of *Argosy*. Jackson's fans immediately wrote letters in his defense, launching a monthly war of words between Jackson supporters and the man who started the controversy. That man was Howard Phillips Lovecraft of Providence, Rhode Island.[1]

Lovecraft's responses were so much more literate than those of Jackson's supporters that his running commentary was noted by Edward F. Daas, Official Editor of the United Amateur Press Association. The UAPA was a loose organization of amateur writers around the country who wrote for or published amateur journals. Daas invited Lovecraft to join the UAPA, and as the op-ed war raged in the pages of *Argosy*, Lovecraft quietly joined the ranks of amateur journalism in April 1914. Lovecraft even became an amateur publisher, producing a magazine, the *Conservative*, of which thirteen issues appeared irregularly between 1915 and 1923.[2] Lovecraft was transforming himself from a passive reader and writer of material for his personal amusement into a writer who could and would influence other readers and writers—with his words, his support, and an unwavering devotion to the English language.

The UAPA had split into two factions after a contentious election at their annual convention in 1912. Daas and other members felt that Helene Hoffman had won the election but had been cheated out of the presidency by parliamentary procedure chicanery. He and those of similar opinion broke away and formed a separate faction, usually referred to as the "Hoffman-Daas" United. It was this UAPA that Lovecraft joined.[3]

Lovecraft embraced the schism-riddled amateur press movement, contributing poetry, stories, essays, and criticism to the publications of various UAPA members with astonishing productivity, starting in July 1914 with an article urging the members to help preserve the language from the scourge of colloquialism and slang. In light of Lovecraft's treatment of Fred Jackson's fiction, it is not surprising that by November 1914, he was made chairman of the UAPA's Department of Public Criticism. His critiques of articles and poetry in the various journals may not always have been kind, but his intent primarily was to help each author improve his or her next endeavor.

Within a year, Lovecraft's reports to the Department of Public Criticism included mention of a new amateur periodical called the *Tryout*. In an autobiographical sketch in 1943, Charles W. Smith recalled how his journal, and by extension he himself, acquired the name *Tryout*:

> About 1911 Edith Miniter wanted me to print a memorial to Susan B. Robbins. I wanted to do it, as I held her in high esteem. But I had no press nor type, and told Edith I couldn't do it. But it kept bobbing up in my mind, and at last I bought an 8 × 10 Pilot Press and type, and the memorial was issued. Having material to print and getting my fingers again in the type case and my hand on the lever of the press, I hated to stop printing. My eyes were bothering me and I didn't think they could stand the strain of setting type. I chawed over the matter some time and thought I can give my eyes a tryout anyway. If I issue a paper I thought, I'll call it Tryout. And that's how Tryout came to be named in 1914. Calling myself Tryout was the suggestion of Howard P. Lovecraft. One of my letters to him was signed Tryout and it pleased him. Since then I have signed all my letters Tryout.[4]

Lovecraft's first submittal to the *Tryout* was "The Power of Wine: A Satire," a poem previously published in a Providence newspaper, and it appeared the April 1916 issue. By the end of 1917, his résumé included more than a dozen poems in the *Tryout* under his name and several aliases. Lovecraft also began sending articles to Smith for publication, starting with an article lambasting a piece in a previous issue by James F. Morton in which Morton had accidentally referred to Persia as being in Europe. This was the start of a working relationship with the *Tryout* that quickly became a friendship with the publisher, Charles W. Smith of Haverhill, Massachusetts.

In 1920, Lovecraft published an essay chronicling the history of amateur journalism. "Looking Backward" ran in the February, March, April, May, and June issues of the *Tryout* and proved popular enough that Lovecraft and Smith reprinted the essay as a 36-page booklet. The *Tryout* was an unofficial arm of the National Amateur Press Association, a rival to Lovecraft's own UAPA faction. Although Lovecraft was active in the UAPA politics and held various offices, he joined the rival National Amateur Press Association at Smith's urging. Except for an unexpected stint as interim president of the group in 1922–23, Lovecraft tried to limit his participation to an occasional convention appearance and contributions to both *Tryout* and the *Vagrant*, which was published by longtime friend W. Paul Cook.

It is in the pages of the *Tryout* that several of Lovecraft's short stories were first published, including "The Cats of Ulthar" (November 1920), "The Terrible Old Man" (July 1921), and "The Tree" (October 1921). *Tryout* also published Lovecraft's non-fiction, and it was where much of Lovecraft's poetry was first published. The poems included several inspired by Smith and by visits to Haverhill, including "Tryout's Lament for the Vanished Spider" (1920) and the elegy "Sir Thomas Tryout" (1921), in memory of Smith's cat. Lovecraft continued to be such a prolific contributor to the *Tryout* that even today, the complete list of *noms de plume* concocted by Smith and Lovecraft remains a mystery.

Charles William Smith was born in Haverhill on 24 October 1852. As a teenager, he was fascinated with typesetting and acquired a small hand press to experiment with on his own. Although he was being paid to print calling cards and other small jobs for friends, even as a teen, Smith considered it a hobby.

Smith attended Haverhill schools, dropping out at thirteen to work in a factory as a stock clerk, not unusual for the times. His father began working in a local sawmill, and Smith and his brother Frank soon joined their father manufacturing wooden boxes at the John Green Box Company at 62 Fleet Street.

After his marriage to Ida Boynton in 1876, Smith lived with his parents at 6 Auburn Street until after the birth of his children. His wife died in 1885, leaving Smith with two preteen daughters. He returned to Auburn Street so that his widowed mother could help to raise his daughters.

In 1888, Frank was too ill to work, so Smith returned to his childhood hobby of printing to help Frank earn something. The brothers began publishing the *Monthly Visitor*, a widely circulated amateur publication that started in December 1888 and issued 118 numbers, the last issue coming off the press in October 1898. Frank would, as his health permitted, look for advertisers while Charles ran the press.[5]

Charles worked his way up to foreman at the box company, eventually buying the company in 1897 from the retiring owner and renaming it the C. W. Smith Box Company. Located across from the back

The Monthly Visitor.

VOL. VII.   HAVERHILL, MASS., MARCH, 1894   NO. 3.

THE ASKING SOUL.

WHY should we fret so?
    Grieve so? regret so?
Turning the blessings of God into bane?
    Making life weary,
    Woeful and dreary,
Spurning the pleasure and pressing the pain.

    Why should we fret so?
    Fear so? forget so?
Shunning the blossom and seeking the thorn?
    Searching for evil,
    Hoarding affection and spreading our scorn?

    Why should we fret so?
    Aid so? abet so?
Doubt and unfaith from the night stealing north
    Let us more wise be,
    Swift to surmise be,
God is in Heaven and peace is on earth.
        A. H. GOODENOUGH.

to attempt mentioning that author's work. The *picture* of the poem is simply exquisite :

"For the whole little hill-town blazed with
        them,
And every girl had a flower to wear,
Hued like a star, or hued like a gem,
Or scarlet flame on a flickering stem,
Or gold as her own gold hair."

J. Rosevelt Gleason's lines entitled :"My Home" has just enough of the indefinable about them to lend them a charm, although we may catch our truant mind in doubting whether

    "Within this sphere
Lies all the love of man."

The closing lines are particularly fine :

"But that fond soaring love of thine
Wing'd like a star for reckless flight,
May yet in brightest beauty shine
On the dark verge of sorrow's night."

Perhaps some prosaic astronomer might question that figure of a star winged for flight. but even the astronomer loses himself sometimes —in poetry like this.

Mr. Emery's Two Rondelaux, complete the issue's contributions. They are Emery-poems—I have nothing further to say concerning them, for, like "Lester Kirk" I have a fashion of merely mention-

Charles W. Smith's *Monthly Visitor* (1888–97), a precursor to the *Tryout*. *Courtesy the Trustees of the Haverhill Public Library, Special Collections Department.*

of Haverhill's City Hall on Main Street, Smith expanded the business to sell the sawdust created in the box-making operation. Smith's business acumen, or at least his timing, was suspect at best. His purchase of the box company coincided with the introduction of less expensive cardboard boxes, and the wooden box industry began to decline.

A 1920 postcard showing the Haverhill B&M railroad station.

In 1899, Smith's box factory suffered a two-alarm blaze that gutted the building. The fires started in an adjoining building but quickly spread to his three-story wooden structure, which was filled with dry wood and sawdust. The conflagration's intensity and proximity to the City Hall undoubtedly raised the specter of the Great Fire of 1882, which had leveled the downtown shoe manufacturing district. The *Boston Daily Globe* noted the mill had been the site of four major fires and the neighborhood of aging wooden industrial structures were among the most dangerous buildings in the city.[6]

The strain of rebuilding after the fire while caring for his mother became too much, and in 1903 Smith suffered an attack of "nervous prostration." The *Monthly Visitor* had ceased publication in 1889 when Tryout discovered owning his business left no time for amateur journalism. Now, with his current health issues, any second thoughts of returning to publishing evaporated; the press was packed away. Smith sold his company to one of his distributors, Osman S. Currier.[7] Smith's mother moved in with her sister, and Tryout moved in with his daughter Susan Britton and her family on Groveland Street. Although the address of 408 Groveland Street has become indelibly connected with Tryout Smith, the house was actually owned by his son-in-law Charles Britton. He himself never owned a house of his own. Smith lived in the Groveland Street house almost uninterruptedly from 1904 until his death.[8]

After a decade of retirement, he dusted off his press and re-entered the world of amateur journalism. The first issue of the *Tryout* was published in 1914 from a shed in the yard in Groveland Street. At the time, Smith was sixty-two years old, mostly deaf from his years in the mill, and further hindered with such poor vision that typesetting became somewhat of an adventure. But he was nothing if not reliable, hand-setting the type for 300 issues from 1914 to 1944. The publication was legendary for its typographical errors, which infuriated contributors unaware of Smith's age and infirmities. Lovecraft, occasionally vexed by the errors but sympathetic as to the reason for them, quaintly referred to them as "tryoutisms."[9]

When Smith's health declined in later years, the press was moved into the house, but by then the shed had been immortalized in Lovecraft's correspondence. In a letter to Rheinhart Kleiner of 1921, Lovecraft described his first visit with Smith in the shed as "a veritable curiosity shop, with all the odds and ends of forty years hung or strewn about. There are buttons, stamps, chromos, and dingy photographs on the walls, and in various corners sundry odd iron objects—a miniature anvil, for instance—washed in by the tides of the neighbouring Merrimack."[10]

Lovecraft described the structure as a "dilapidated old cottage" or "a pleasant cottage,"[11] depending on when and to whom he was writing. The shed, and later the house, eventually were destroyed.[12]

As Smith was printing the final installment of "Looking Backward" in the June 1920 issue of the *Tryout*, Lovecraft was visited in Providence, Rhode Island, by Edward F. Daas. It may have been Daas who suggested the article be reprinted as a booklet. But whatever their discussions entailed, it precipitated another transformation in Lovecraft.

Although Lovecraft received visitors in his home, he was virtually a recluse. After the visit from Daas, he decided to travel. Part of this sudden interest in travel may have been his mother's nervous breakdown. When Susan was hospitalized in 1919, it removed the doting and over-protectiveness that had isolated Lovecraft from the world.

His first trip was to Boston for a gathering of amateur journalists. It was not difficult. Lovecraft was accompanied by several UAPA members from New York who had arrived in Providence the previous day; the trip simply involved catching the New York, New Haven & Hartford Railroad at Union Station with experienced train passengers and riding the train to Boston's South Station. A simple excursion but, as Lovecraft later admitted to Edwin Baird in a 1924 letter, it was the first time he had not slept at home since he was a lad of eleven, back in 1901![13]

Tryout Smith (1852–1948), as photographed at his type case in 1942 by his grandson Daniel Pond. *Courtesy Kenneth W. Faig, Jr.*

After embarking on two more trips to Boston in 1920 and another two early in 1921, it appeared Lovecraft had become comfortable in social settings. So in May, he prepared for his most ambitious trip to date. At the invitation of a correspondent, Lovecraft began planning a visit to the Merrimack Valley.

Chapter 2
First Visits: 1921

In May 1921, Lovecraft was finalizing plans for a two-day trip to Hampstead, New Hampshire. His hostess was to be Miss Myrta Alice Little, who lived with her family on a farm that had been in her family since the colonial era.

Of the correspondence between Little and Lovecraft, only a single letter survives, that of 17 May from Lovecraft asking for guidance as to which train station he should take—Westville or Hampstead. The tone of the text suggests that Lovecraft and Little had been corresponding for some time. Lovecraft mentions Little's "domestic upheaval" (she had just returned to Hampstead from two years working in Sacramento, California), updates on his health, his delight that she had made contact with his long-time correspondent Alfred Galpin, and similar diverse topics that reflect a letter typical of those to his regular correspondents.[1]

Little was a budding professional writer who dabbled briefly in the UAPA. She was appearing in the *Tryout* by the November 1920 issue (which contained Lovecraft's short story "The Cats of Ulthar"). S. T. Joshi suggests that Lovecraft and Little may have met through Tryout Smith.[2] Lovecraft had been corresponding with Smith since 1917. He could have met Little as early as 1915, when she was an instructor at

Myrta Alice Little in 1908 as a senior at Colby College, Maine.

the Rhode Island Normal School in Providence for one semester and attending classes at Brown University. The YWCA on Washington Street where she stayed was a mile west of Brown. At the time, Lovecraft lived on Angell Street a mile to the east. The first contact between them that can be confirmed is the listing of Little as a "new recruit" in the November 1920 "News Notes" of the *United Amateur,* then edited by Lovecraft.[3]

Lovecraft does not mention Little in his surviving correspondence until 1921, after the first visit to Hampstead.[4] It is interesting to note that when Lovecraft married Sonia Greene in 1924, he informed no one about the impending nuptials until after the fact. This reticence to share his visit to New Hampshire before the fact may similarly indicate that Lovecraft preferred to keep parts of his private life (and any potential romances) to himself; or it may simply be another gap in the timeline.

This raises the question: Did Little begin corresponding with Lovecraft because they both appeared in the same issue of the *Tryout,* or because Lovecraft was an officer of the UAPA at the time she joined the organization, or because they had known each other in Providence? Regardless of when or how they first met, evidence suggests Little became a regular correspondent for a number of years. Although the sole surviving letter is from 1921, an envelope addressed by Lovecraft to Little postmarked 1927 appeared at auction, and in 1937, R. H. Barlow copied her name and address from Lovecraft's address book.[5]

Myrta Alice Little was a card-carrying member of the DAR, with a lineage back to the founding of Haverhill in 1640. She had only just returned to Hampstead after extensive traveling in pursuit of her career as a teacher. As part of her senior requirements from Maine's Colby College, she taught in Proctor, Vermont, for a semester. With her B.A. in hand, she moved to Oxford, Massachusetts, and taught for two years. Returning to Radcliffe for an M.A., she headed the English Department at New York's Alfred University for a year while the department head was on sabbatical, then continued on at Alfred as an associate professor of English and public speaking. Little resigned the position to prepare for a new challenge with even more travel. She accepted a teaching position at the American College for Girls in Constantinople.

Little returned to Hampstead only to see the Constantinople job abruptly vaporize when Turkey bombed Russian ports on the Black Sea on 28 October 1914 and entered World War I. Instead, Little took the first available opening, the Rhode Island State Normal School in Providence. After a semester there, she continued to travel, first to Norton, Massachusetts, to teach at Wheaton College, and then to serve two years as the educational secretary for the YWCA in Sacramento, California.

By 1919, Little had tired of moving from job to job and decided to become a writer. She returned to Hampstead and found immediate professional success writing short fiction for the McClure Newspaper Syndicate, as well as contributions to amateur journals such as the *Tryout*.

In May 1921, Lovecraft had decided to accept Little's invitation to visit her and her family in Hampstead. The plan was to arrive on 8 June, stay overnight, and then take the train to Boston in time for an amateur press meeting. The plans were placed in jeopardy when, on 24 May, Lovecraft's mother died unexpectedly. Susan Lovecraft's death put her son into a depression that he was unable to shake. Finally, his aunts insisted he take up the offer to visit New Hampshire as a way to stir him from his malaise. Lovecraft acquiesced.

On 8 June, he boarded the New York, New Haven & Hartford Railroad in Providence, arrived in Boston, and transferred to the Boston & Maine train. Four and a half hours after leaving Providence, Lovecraft arrived at the Westville Depot in Plaistow, New Hampshire.

Westville Depot was hardly a train station. Trains stopped at the one-room building only if someone was getting on or off, usually locals commuting to or from Haverhill to work at the shoe factories. The nearby general store doubled as the Westville post office. In addition to meeting the Little family at the station, Lovecraft used the post office at least once to deposit his constant stream of outgoing mail.[6]

Hampstead was incorporated in 1749. The contested boundary between Massachusetts and New Hampshire was finally settled in 1739, and the northernmost parts of Haverhill and Amesbury found themselves north of the line. At the time of Lovecraft's visit, the town was a typical small New England village, with farms and mills centered on a small downtown. Almost the entire population of 1250 could trace their lineages back to the original settlers of the Merrimack Valley.

No details are known of that first day of Lovecraft's first visit to the 150-year-old Colonial farmhouse, but a letter to Frank Belknap Long in 1922 recalled this and subsequent visits, indicating how well the Little family knew their guest: "knowing my archaic tastes, they always assign me a room in the unrestored part—where I sleep on a four-poster bed and under blankets all made in the eighteenth century."[7]

The second day of the visit is well documented. In his May letter to Myrta Little, Lovecraft had lamented how unfortunate it was that Tryout Smith did not feet well enough to receive visitors. By the time Lovecraft arrived, Smith apparently had changed his mind, and it was now Lovecraft's intention to visit Smith in Haverhill on the second day of his trip.

When Little learned that Lovecraft planned to meet the fabled printer, she asked to accompany him. The result was a two-hour visit with Smith on Groveland Street that Lovecraft dutifully recorded for publication as "The Haverhill Convention" in the next edition of the *Tryout*.[8]

Settled in 1640 as Pentucket and renamed for the English birthplace of first minister John Ward, Haverhill's location on the Merrimack River guaranteed that the colonial farming village would grow into a mill city as the industrial revolution arose, powered by the endless water of the Merrimack. By the 1830s, Haverhill was becoming known for shoe manufacturing. The demands of outfitting the troops during the Civil War propelled the city into the role of a leader in the industry, and Haverhill was soon a major force in both domestic and international shoe production with tanneries, shoe factories, and design companies lining the riverbank along Merrimack Street and spilling onto Washington Street. By 1880, virtually the entire shoe industry had consolidated in the area. The proximity became a liability on the night of 17 February 1882, when a fire leveled ten acres of the shoe district. Within months, the area was rebuilding and sturdy brick

The John Ward House.

structures replaced the charred ruins of wooden structures. The rebuilt Washington Street became the center of the shoe trade, with a street lined with buildings of Queen Anne industrial architecture.

By 1913, one out of every ten pairs of shoes in America was produced in Haverhill, and the city proclaimed itself to be the "Queen Slipper City of the World." The glory did not last; after World War I the domestic shoe industry faced growing competition from foreign manufacturers. The shoe industry was just beginning a gradual but inexorable decline in Haverhill when Lovecraft arrived with Little.

"The Haverhill Convention" is a tongue-in-cheek account of the first two-hour visit of Lovecraft, Tryout Smith, and Myrta Little. Buried beneath the sylvan dialogue and description of the shed is Lovecraft's sincere affection for the elderly printer. Additional details of the visit are provided in a letter to Rheinhart Kleiner dated June 12:

> Smith is a lean, wiry man of medium stature & good features, with a short iron-grey beard, a good head of iron-grey hair & a bronzed weather-beaten complexion gained by his outdoor programme. He wears old clothes—which sit neatly on his active frame—& has a pleasant voice with a somewhat rural accent. His deafness is no obstacle to conversation if one speaks incisively & near his ear. He confesses to *69* years, but does not look a day over 50. In person he bears

out every impression which one gains from the *Tryout*—I like him immeasurably, for he is the most unspoiled, simple, contented, artless, and altogether delightful small boy of his age that I have ever beheld. He never grew up, but lives on without any of the dull complexities of adulthood—active, busy with his little press, stamp album, cat, and woodland excursions.[9]

The first day in Hampstead is glossed over in favor of the highlights of the visit to Tryout Smith in Haverhill. Between the letter and the essay, Lovecraft crafts a description of the shed on Groveland Street as an eclectic patchwork of Smith's collections of postcards, stamps, buttons, photographs, and assorted detritus recovered on the riverbank. Long before actually meeting Tryout, Lovecraft had remarked about Smith's most avid hobby outside amateur journalism:

> He is an ardent stamp collector, and has acquired an enormous number of uncancelled postals and stamped envelopes of ancient vintage, which he sometimes uses. A short time ago, he used an 1880 envelope in writing me. A card I received from him yesterday is a relic of the 1890s.[10]

At the time of the visit, Smith was setting the type for the July issue of the *Tryout,* featuring the debut of Lovecraft's short story "The Terrible Old Man."[11] Lovecraft also met Tryout's cats, Tom and "The Mascot." Tom, spooked by the visitors, avoided the new arrivals, and Lovecraft feigned indignation at the feline snub "after the verse that I have dedicated to him."[12] The visit was considered a great success and Little exacted a promise from Lovecraft to return for another visit. That visit would turn out to be sooner than expected. Lovecraft returned to Hampstead in August of the same year.

In a letter to Alfred Galpin dated 31 August 1921,[13] Lovecraft recounts being met at the Haverhill B&M railroad station on 25 August by Myrta Little and several family members in their "horseless carriage." After stopping at Smith's residence and not finding him at home, the Littles drove Lovecraft to local landmark Winnekenni Castle.[14] Lovecraft apparently was impressed with the two-story fieldstone edifice with a three-story turret, overlooking Kenoza Lake. He referred to the castle as picturesque and would not have been surprised to see a ghostly knight on patrol. The Littles then drove Lovecraft to Hampstead. Arriving at the Little farmhouse, Lovecraft wrote of a new experience to his aunt. He had picked strawberries, which he admits he had never actually seen growing on the vine.[15]

Winnekenni Castle. *Courtesy Joan Goudsward.*

The next day found Lovecraft reading some of his new stories to the Little family. One story in particular, "The Outsider," drew a suggestion from the family. Lovecraft agreed with the critique and implemented the change. The story would not appear in print for another five years (in *Weird Tales,* April 1926).[16]

The Buttonwoods, home of the Haverhill Historical Society.

The afternoon plan was to try again to visit Smith and then to explore the nearby Haverhill Historical Society. Tryout was home and eagerly awaiting his visitors. He had been napping the previous day; that and his deafness had caused him to miss his callers. The visit was brief, but Little reiterated a promise from the previous visit to bake Tryout a gingerbread cake in thanks for his hospitality.

Little and Lovecraft then proceed to the "The Buttonwoods," the museum of the Haverhill Historical Society. He wrote to his aunt, Annie Phillips Gamwell:

> The greatest event was the visit to the Historical Society, which is housed in a museum attached to the ancestral mansion of the director. The latter place is itself a museum—all the more interesting because it is the natural collection of a family rather than the artificial collection of an institution. The director—a Mr. Leonard Smith—is an elderly man of vast refinement & scholarship. Yesterday was not a visiting day, but since the Littles are personally acquainted with important personages of the Society, we were allowed to go through the collection. Mr. Smith—as delightful in a patrician way as C. W. Smith is in a plebeian way—personally guided the tour, sharing his house & landscape gardens as well as the museum. On the grounds is another small house—the oldest in Haverhill—built in 1640. It is the oldest house I have ever seen or entered."[17]

The small house Lovecraft refers to is the John Ward House. At the time of his visit, the structure was thought to date to the founding of Haverhill in 1640s as the home of Haverhill's first minister, John Ward. It has since been determined that the wooden-framed building is not as old as believed; the eastern half dates only to 1720, the western half to 1800. The building stands on its original site, from which it had been removed in 1882 and then returned in 1906 when acquired by the museum.

Myrta Little's DAR credentials were through her colonial blood-lines, as she was descended from the venerable Peaslees of Haverhill and also a third great-granddaughter of Josiah Bartlett, a signer of the Declaration of Independence in New Hampshire. She was considered somewhat of a blueblood in local historical circles and allowed membership in several somewhat exclusive Haverhill women's groups. Little also possessed a certain cachet at the historical society, which allowed her to arrange a visit to the museum on a day it was not normally open to the public. This idea of gaining access to a historical society on such a day apparently impressed Lovecraft to the point that he would include a similar incident in 1931 when writing "The Shadow over Innsmouth."

Returning to Hampstead, Lovecraft planned to go stargazing behind the Little house, on a summit locally known as "The Pinnacle." Today the exact location of the Pinnacle is unknown. The name has slipped into obscurity as properties changed hands and local nomenclature faded from use. The most logical choice is an unnamed hill directly behind the Little homestead that rises 340 feet in elevation.[18] In a letter to his aunt, Lovecraft recounts taking his field glasses and planisphere and climbing the hill with a flashlight, only to be thwarted by the cloud cover.[19]

The next morning, Lovecraft used binoculars to view the land-scape, waxing poetic to Galpin about viewing the town spires through the trees. After lunch, Lovecraft assisted Little in the kitchen as they baked the promised gingerbread for Smith, which Lovecraft dutifully carried on his lap in the car to Haverhill, delivering it to Smith before catching the train to Boston.[20]

The Little Family Homestead as it appeared in Hampstead's 200th Anniversary souvenir booklet, 1949.

It would be another nine months before Lovecraft would return to the Merrimack Valley, but in that time changes were taking place. Little was elected historian of the UAPA even as she continued to build an extensive résumé of paid professional writing. Her future husband, the Reverend Arthur Robert Davies arrived in Derry to lead the local Methodist Church.

Tryout Smith continued to print a new issue of the *Tryout* each month like clockwork, but his sanctuary on Groveland Street was under siege. His daughter Susan Britton had died in 1920, leaving her husband Charles, an infant, a seven-year old daughter, and two adult sons. Charles's parents and his brother William moved in to help. The crowded situation on Groveland Street began to aggravate Tryout's nervous condition.

Lovecraft gained yet another new correspondent in amateur journalism, Edgar Jacobs Davis, who lived in the town of Merrimac, Massachusetts, just east of Haverhill. He would stop in Merrimac for a brief visit when he returned to visit Myrta Little and her family in May 1922. The stay in Hampstead was brief, and few details are recorded in Lovecraft's letters. The Littles were packing for a visit to their summer camp on Lake Winnipesaukee, so Lovecraft used the opportunity to head into Haverhill, presumably with a brief visit to Tryout, and a trolley ride to Merrimac to see Edgar J. Davis.

Merrimac was primarily a residential community, but not necessarily by choice. The town was once a center for the carriage-making industry. The town's very existence was a result of the carriages. When West Amesbury and East Amesbury began squabbling over the carriage industry, the towns split. East Amesbury became Amesbury and concentrated on mass-produced, lower-priced carriages, whereas West Amesbury became Merrimac and concentrated on higher-end, customizable carriages such as the landau. When the automobile replaced the carriage, Amesbury dabbled in auto bodies before falling back on textile mills. Merrimac had no other industries to soften the blow.

Edgar Davis (1908–1949) began corresponding with Lovecraft soon after recruitment into the UAPA in March 1922. Lovecraft replied to Davis's letters, aware that his correspondent was a gifted thirteen-year old.[21] Davis was born in Haverhill on 21 April 1908, the son of Herman F. Davis, a hardware salesman, and Harriet D. Jacobs, a former school teacher. Soon after his birth, his father opened what would be the first in a small chain of retail hardware stores in the Greater Haverhill area.

Edgar's fascination with writing led him to the amateur press movement and subsequent correspondence with Lovecraft. In a letter to Samuel Loveman in 1923, Lovecraft mentions another visit to Merrimac and expresses some sympathy for Edgar because, although his mother and sister supported his studies, his father was more practical and thought little of his son's scholarly and artistic endeavors.[22] As it would turn out, this caused Edgar's amateur submittals to be all but impossible to locate, and he never pursued a professional career.

The first Merrimac trip was a brief visit, but Edgar managed to find something of interest for his guest. The Davis home was within walking distance of the Old Sawyer House, a colonial New England saltbox owned by the same family from 1758 to 1908, when it was sold to a local historical society. The house retains much of its original paneling and upstairs windows, although the downstairs fireplaces were renovated in the mid-nineteenth century.

Lovecraft was impressed enough to mention the visit to his aunt Lillian Clark and to refer to the building in a letter[23] to his aunt in September 1922 discussing a visit to the Morris-Jumel Mansion in Manhattan. He noted gleefully that when he signed the guest register at the New York historic house museum that served as the headquarters of both British and American forces at different points in the war, he did so as a loyal English subject before the Revolution, signing as "H: Lovecraft, Gent., Providence-Plantations, in Rd: Island" just as he had signed the register at the Sawyer House in May.

In 1924, in a letter to Frank Belknap Long,[24] Lovecraft mentions Exeter, New Hampshire, as one of a handful of towns that maintained its colonial buildings so well that he could scarcely believe he was not in the eighteenth century. Exeter is also home to Phillips Exeter Academy, founded in 1781 by merchant John Phillips, who Lovecraft erroneously believed was a distant relative on his mother's side. This John was the great-great-grandson of Reverend George Phillips (1593?–1644) of Watertown, Massachusetts. Lovecraft had identified Reverend Phillips as the North American progenitor of his mother's Phillips line. The genealogy goes astray after his great-great-great grandfather Asaph Phillips.[25] Lovecraft never specifically notes when he made a visit to

The Old Sawyer House museum (c.1735).

Exeter to make such an observation, but circumstantial evidence places the visit at the end of his stay in Hampstead in May 1922.

When the Littles departed for their summer camp on Lake Winnipesaukee, Lovecraft accompanied them as far as Dover, New Hampshire, where he caught the train back to Boston. The automobile route, considering the limited number of paved roads, would suggest a route from Hampstead to Kingston and then on to Exeter.

Although from Exeter, it was just 20 miles straight up the Exeter Road into Dover, Lovecraft mentions in the same letter that he had caught sight of Maine but didn't actually enter the state. This suggests that the Littles, knowing Lovecraft's antiquarian interests, went east instead of north, taking the state route now designated Route 108/33 into Portsmouth, which they could connect to State Route 16 and then Dover.

Portsmouth became a favorite city for Lovecraft and he would return several times to explore its ancient buildings, but it would be his

The Davis family home off Merrimac Square.

last visit to Hampstead. By the time Lovecraft was planning his next trip to the Merrimack Valley, Myrta Little was already engaged to marry Arthur Davies of neighboring Derry, New Hampshire.

But as the door to the Little house was closing, Edgar Davis and his family were encouraging Lovecraft to come for another visit. This visit would include a new destination that would inspire one of Lovecraft's most famous creations—the blighted village of Innsmouth.

Chapter 3
WHITTIERLAND AND NEWBURYPORT

If there had been any potential for romance between Little and Love-craft, it was doomed from the start. Little's life and career choices reflected a search for spirituality, starting with being the youngest person ever admitted to full membership at Hampstead's Congregational Church. Her positions included teaching at Alfred University (Seventh Day Adventists) and Wheaton College (nondenominational Christian). She worked for the YWCA in California. Had the war not interrupted her plans, she would have been teaching in Constantinople, at a college for girls that aimed at serving the Christian minorities. The ceremony for her marriage to a Methodist minister was performed by Dr. Francis Strickland, an early figure in the Emmanuel Movement, a psychologically based approach to religious healing. Lovecraft, conversely, was an avowed atheist who included a parody of insipid Sunday school exempla, "'George's Sacrifice' By Percy Vacuum, age 8," in his one surviving letter to Little.[1]

In 1922, Tryout Smith had suffered another attack of nervous prostration and under doctor's orders was convalescing in Plaistow, New Hampshire. Smith would remain in Plaistow until 1926. His home with his late daughter Susan Britton's family on Groveland Street was severely overcrowded, as Smith's other daughter Jennie, Charles Britton's parents, and his brother moved in as well. The number of occupants at Groveland Street suddenly went from three adults and three children in 1920 to ten people in 1923: five adults, two adult children, two children, and a live-in maid. Adding to the chaos was the inherent disruption that comes with planning a wedding: Tryout's oldest grandson Truman was getting married. Tryout could not handle the stress. Under a doctor's order to get some tranquility back into his life, he moved to Plaistow where his son-in-law owned a farmhouse.[2] The solitude gave rise to boredom and before long, Smith moved his press to Plaistow and the *Tryout* resumed publication, with the numbering resuming where it had left off. He refused all invitations to accompany Lovecraft on his travels and he took no visitors at his rural retreat.

In April 1923, Lovecraft embarked on another round of travel, starting in Salem and Danvers where he explored houses associated with the witch trials before catching the train to Haverhill.[3] This time there was no one at the station in Railroad Square to meet him. Myrta Little was less than two weeks from marrying Arthur Davies, a transplanted Methodist minister from upstate New York whose pastorate was now Derry.

Postcard of Washington Street c. 1895, looking toward Washington Square and Merrimack Street from Railroad Square.

So in Haverhill, Lovecraft hopped the trolley in Washington Square and headed to neighboring Merrimac to see Edgar Davis. Having arrived on one of the trains from Boston, Lovecraft would find himself at the depot in Railroad Square. Less than a quarter-mile down Washington Street is Washington Square, the nexus for trolley lines heading toward locales where he was planning to visit his correspondents. The line east to Newburyport via Amesbury would bring Lovecraft to the door of Edgar J. Davis in Merrimac. He could also board a bus at the stop in Washington Square, in front of the Coombs Building.

In 1976, the road Lovecraft had walked from train to trolley was added to the National Register of Historic Places as the Washington Street Shoe District, one of the finest examples of a complete street of Queen Anne industrial architecture in America.

The goal of Lovecraft's trip in 1923 was to tour Newburyport as part of his antiquarian wanderings. By the time he arrived in Merrimac and at the Davis house, it was afternoon, and too late to set off exploring Newburyport. Instead, Davis and Lovecraft boarded the trolley to Amesbury to explore the haunts of John Greenleaf Whittier.

Whittier (1807–1892) was an influential Quaker poet. Although best remembered for his abolitionist stance and his poems celebrating rural life, Whittier also knew enough local folklore tales of deviltry and the supernatural to add to his poetry and to publish books on the topic: *The Legends of New England* (1831) and *The Supernaturalism of New England* (1847).

He was born in Haverhill at the family farm, built in 1688 and home to five generations of Whittiers. Located off Amesbury Road (Route 110), the farmhouse would have become a familiar sight on Lovecraft's trolley rides to Merrimac from Haverhill.

In a letter later that month to his friend Samuel Loveman, Lovecraft chronicles his first visit to Newburyport, mentioning the side trip to Amesbury to explore the local Whittier home, gravesite, and "other typical reliquiae."[4]

From 1836 until his death in 1892, John Greenleaf Whittier lived and wrote most of his poetry and prose at his home on Friend Street in Amesbury. Built circa 1829, the house is a National Historic Landmark.

The oldest section of Union Cemetery is located near the spot of the first Meeting House in Amesbury, erected in 1665. The cemetery absorbed neighboring Bartlett Cemetery (est. 1888) and the Society of Friends Cemetery, which traditionally has no markers. Quaker or not, Lovecraft and Davis found the headstone they sought. Whittier is in a family plot in the Society of Friends section, along with other family members commemorated in "Snow Bound." The simple headstone is

The Whittier ancestral family home (built 1688) in East Haverhill.

not hard to find, as ample signage leads to it.

About 500 feet from Whittier's final resting place is the headstone of Captain Valentine Bagley (1773–1839), the subject of Whittier's "The Captain's Well," another of the Whittier landmarks visited by Lovecraft. Located on Main Street, the well was immortalized by Whittier in a poem telling the story of the shipwreck of Amesbury native Bagley on the coast of Arabia. Bagley suffered from thirst in the desert, so he vowed to dig a well in order that no man should suffer from thirst as he did. Lovecraft notes that the well was among his stops in his afternoon tour of Amesbury. Whittier's poem was first published in his collection *At Sundown* (1890).

Lovecraft and Davis returned to Merrimac, where Lovecraft spent the night debating with Edgar's father, Herman. The next day would herald the start of the object of the visit—Lovecraft's first visit to Newburyport.

Oliver Wendell Holmes may have been the reason for Lovecraft's visit to Newburyport. Lovecraft's earliest recollections included meeting Oliver Wendell Holmes in 1892 as a two-year-old while vacationing with his parents. He professed a "marked prejudice in his favour."[5] This would include familiarity with Holmes's *Elsie Venner: A Romance of Destiny*, a book Lovecraft would mention in "Supernatural

Horror in Literature" as having "with admirable restraint an unnatural ophidian element in a young woman prenatally influenced, and sustains the atmosphere with finely discriminating landscape touches."[6]

Newburyport was settled in 1635 as part of Newberry Plantation, now Newbury. Situated at the mouth of the Merrimack River, it quickly became a fishing, shipbuilding, and shipping center. The shipowners of Newburyport grew wealthy, courtesy of the infamous triangular trade, slaves to molasses to rum. It would not last. Newburyport was hit hard by Jefferson's Embargo Act of 1807 against Great Britain and France. The waterfront was destroyed in a fire in 1811, and the war of 1812 shut down trade with Europe. By 1820, the port had silted in; at the time of the Civil War, Newburyport and Portsmouth, another Lovecraft favorite, in the words of Oliver Wendell Holmes, Sr., was of "weakened, but not impoverished, gentility." He does further note that

> It is not with any thought of pity or depreciation that we speak of them as in a certain sense decayed towns; they did not fulfil their early promise of expansion, but they remain incomparably the most interesting places of their size in any of the three northernmost New England States.[7]

On the morning of 15 April, Lovecraft and Davis departed on the trolley for Newburyport but without Tryout Smith. While regaining his equilibrium, Smith still refused all visitors and attempts to include him in adventures; several of Lovecraft's letters of 1923 note with regret Smith's disinclination to tag along.[8] The trolley took them through Amesbury, crossing the Merrimack River at Deer Island on the Chain Bridge.[9] Lovecraft mentions the bridge in his letters,[10] but he does not mention that the trolley went directly past the only residence on Deer Island, the former home of authoress Harriet Prescott Spofford, who had died two years before.[11] This omission is no oversight: when Lovecraft wrote "Supernatural Horror in Literature" between 1925 and 1927, he chose not to mention her contributions in the field.[12] He had once told a correspondent, "I seem to recall reading many things by Harriet Prescott Spofford in youth—things of a very conventional & innocuous nature."[13]

The "Captain's Well," dug by Valentine Bagley.

Home of John Greenleaf Whittier.

As the two entered Newburyport along Merrimack Street, they paralleled the river. The one glimmer of industry still operating on Merrimack Street that Lovecraft would have seen was a battered wooden mill building. Chase Shawmut was a manufacturer of electrical couplings and circuit breakers. After a fire destroyed the company's building in Boston in 1902, Chase Shawmut purchased the old Bayley Hat factory on Merrimack Street and resumed operations. Bayley Hat Company had been established in 1863, meaning when Lovecraft passed the building, it was a sixty-year-old wooden building that backed along the Merrimack River and was showing the effects of New England weather along a river at the edge of the ocean.

This building would become the Marsh Refinery of Innsmouth, a decrepit old mill on the lower part of the Manuxet River where it passes through Innsmouth. Despite the condition of the building, the local economy, and an apparent lack of activity in the mill, it is the sole remaining industry in Innsmouth other than fishing.[14]

In a letter to Loveman after the trip, Lovecraft describes the approach to Newburyport:

> we approached the suburbs of Newburyport & began to get whiffs & glimpses of the neighbouring sea, & to descry the ancient houses & chimney-pots of the famous town which, though said a century and a quarter ago to possess a social life more cultivated & brilliant than that of Washington, is today locally known as the "City of the Living Dead."[15]

Lovecraft and Davis planned to ride the trolley into the center of town and then set out exploring on foot. After riding past a collection of old brick commercial buildings, they realized that the scenery was taking a turn away from the urban. The conglomeration of old brick factory buildings, as they would soon discover, was Market Square, the center of downtown. They were now heading away from downtown, toward Plum Island along on Water Street, past the collection of battered clam digger shanties known as Joppa Flats or colloquially as "Old Joppy." They disembarked from the trolley and walked back toward Market Square, soaking in the panoramic view of antique houses. From Market Square they set out for High Street, a street to which he would return on subsequent visits. Lovecraft was not just casually sightseeing; he was looking specifically for number 201 High Street, former home of Timothy Dexter.

"Lord" Timothy Dexter (1747–1806) was one of Newburyport's most famous residents and certainly among the most eccentric. Dexter made his fortune through such improbable investments as shipping

The Chase Shawmut mill. *Courtesy: Newburyport Archival Center at the Newburyport Public Library.*

Newburyport's Market Square, c. 1912. *Courtesy of the Newburyport Archival Center at the Newburyport Public Library.*

42,000 bedwarmer pans to the West Indies, where they sold quickly—not to warm the sheets of Caribbean beds, but to serve as long-handled ladles in the molasses trade. Dexter's house reflected eccentricities as well, and possibly revenge at the local bluebloods who snubbed his unwelcome arrival among the moneyed elite of High Street.

After purchasing a three-story Georgian house on High Street, Dexter added minarets along the roofline and a cupola to the peak, perching a gilded eagle on top. He then erected high pedestals along the street side of the house and had a local woodcarver create wooden statues of great men such as Washington, John Jay, and King George.

With a little paint and the whims of Dexter, the identities of his statues were subject to change. Drake's *New England Legends and Folk-Lore* notes the transformation of Captain Henry Morgan into Napoleon Bonaparte, a tale that Lovecraft gleefully repeats to Galpin.[16]

A postcard c. 1905 showing the clam shacks of the Joppa Flats and a trolley passing through the area

Lovecraft notes in a letter to Loveman that his family owned a print of the Dexter house dating to 1810 that showed Dexter's statuary collection. The story of Dexter resonated with Lovecraft, and he would mention Dexter repeatedly in his correspondence. In a letter to Helen Sully in 1933, he still reckoned the High Street house a sight in Newburyport not to miss.[17] By 1923, the statuary was long gone and all that remained under the new owners was the gilt eagle still atop the cupola.

The home of "Lord" Timothy Dexter, built in 1771 and shown here c. 1810. *Courtesy Newburyport Archival Center at the Newburyport Public Library.*

A 1920 postcard showing the original Haverhill Public Library building on Summer Street.

Lovecraft and Davis explored the rest of High Street, noting the construction of the bell tower of St. Paul's Episcopal Church. Lovecraft was elated to see the new steeple being constructed of stone in a Georgian style replacing a "horribly out of place" "gothick monstrosity" that had been gutted by fire in 1920. The new church would be completed and dedicated later that year. In the gravestones around the church, Davis found several stones of his Jacobs and Adams ancestors.[18]

The dropping temperatures announced the end of the day, and the two headed back toward Market Square. They stopped at the century-old Adams House on Inn Street, off Market Square, one of the oldest streets in a city of old streets—narrow and crowded with small wooden and brick buildings of varying states of disrepair. Today, courtesy of an urban renewal grant in the 1970s, it is a brick street for pedestrian traffic, filled with upscale shops. In Lovecraft's time, the Adams House was more of a tenement for blue-collar residents than an inn. The Adams House Café remained viable, and it was there that Lovecraft and Davis ate dinner at "the one decent restaurant" in Newburyport for 65¢ apiece before catching the trolley back to Merrimac.

The evening at the Davis house was spent in usual good-natured debate between Lovecraft and Herman Davis. The next morning, Edgar rushed off to high school while Lovecraft planned to take the train and double back to Marblehead, which he had skipped because of time constraints. He and Edgar's parents continued the previous night's discussion until lunchtime. Herman, whose hardware store chain was still primarily situated in Haverhill, offered to drive Lovecraft to the train station. With insufficient time to reach Marblehead and explore it properly, Lovecraft accepted the ride to Haverhill. Now with some spare time, Lovecraft decided to explore on his own. At his request, Davis dropped him off at the public library on Summer Street.

A letter to Galpin and Frank Belknap Long offers a hint as to the route Herman Davis took. After reiterating his fondness for Winnekenni Castle and the surrounding park from the previous visit,[19] Lovecraft hypothesized that because Haverhill had essentially had been built up since the 1870s, the missing colonial neighborhoods were being compensated for by building in medieval styles, specifically

Winnekenni Castle and another building he saw under construction, a "Gothic monastery" that the new country club was building to use as the clubhouse. Lovecraft was correct as to the Gothic lines of the clubhouse, but subsequent completion of the club in 1925 showed not a monastery but an English Tudor half-timber manor house.

The new Haverhill Country Club clubhouse being built in 1925. *Courtesy of the Trustees of the Haverhill Public Library, Special Collections Department.*

Arriving at the library, Lovecraft spent the afternoon looking up local history and discovered the library's holdings included *A Pickle for the Knowing Ones: or Plain Truth in a Homespun Dress*, Timothy Dexter's famous booklet. Lovecraft probably read the 1838 reprint of the booklet, which remains in the library's holdings. He enjoyed the booklet's humor and Dexter's political views, which resonated with Lovecraft's anti-Wilson sentiments to the point that he copied down a passage from *Pickle* and quoted it in a latter to Galpin.[20]

Lovecraft also read the monthly *Bulletin of the Haverhill Public Library*, the April 1923 issue of which featured an article on an eighteenth-century landscape designer. With his affection for that time period, Lovecraft took a handful of the free bulletins and sent them to his correspondents.[21] Lovecraft took an afternoon train into Boston and then transferred to Providence. He considered the trip exhausting but delightful.

St. Paul's Episcopal Church, completed in 1923. *Courtesy of St. Paul's Church.*

Nine days later, Myrta Little was married in Dorchester to Arthur Davies. Little would remain a casual correspondent of Lovecraft but was not referred to again by Lovecraft in letters to his fellow epistolarians. Whether Little was no longer actively pursuing Lovecraft as a possible suitor or because the newlywed had drifted away from amateur journalism is moot. Her influence on Lovecraft's travels remained.

In May, Lovecraft sent a letter to James F. Morton filled with typical discussions and updates and an incredulous report that Edgar Davis had just sent him a *ninety*-page letter from Merrimac. The student was already emulating the master's prolific letter writing.[22]

In a letter to Maurice W. Moe dated August 1923, Lovecraft recounts his first visit to the city that had so intrigued him during his final visit with Myrta Little back in 1921 that he had immediately planned a trip to explore it further—Portsmouth, New Hampshire. Lovecraft was beyond entranced with the town. He professed that Portsmouth's antiquity surpassed that of his beloved Salem and challenged Marblehead as his favorite destination for antiquarian sight seeing.

> Vistas of endless ancient roofs, steeples, and chimneys, with not a modern feature in sight! Labyrinths of quiet streets and lanes lined with Colonial doorways and innocent of sidewalk or paving—streets redolent of an elder world, and communicating their old-Yankee air to inhabitants.[23]

For his self-professed fondness for the city, his correspondence yields few specifics as to locations he visited on this and subsequent trips. And a trip to Portsmouth would include a stop in Haverhill and Newburyport.

Lovecraft did not visit the Merrimack Valley again until 1927, but the impact of the visit would linger. His return trip included repeat trips to Newburyport, Portsmouth, and Haverhill. By 1927, Little's marriage was not the only change that took place before Lovecraft again visited the region.

BULLETIN
OF THE
HAVERHILL PUBLIC LIBRARY

Vol. 7. No. 24   April, 1923   For Free
                                                         Distribution

HUMPHREY REPTON
Landscape Gardener
1752—1818

HE term "landscape gardener" is significant when applied to Humphrey Repton in that it distinguishes him from the group of "architectural gardeners" which preceded him. Down to the last half of the 18th century, the prevailing style of laying out the grounds that surround a house had been that known as Architectural, sometimes called Geometrical or Regular. Whatever the title, the underlying idea was that of considering the grounds as one with the house, part of a comprehensive scheme designed by the architect and following the lines of the buildings. At the time of Repton the passing of the architectural style was in evidence, greatly influenced, no doubt, by Pope, Addison, and other contemporary writers. Pope killed the fashion of shorn shrubs in his satirical paper No. 173 of the Guardian and Addison voiced the same feeling in his paper on the "Pleasure of a Garden" in No. 477 of the Spectator papers. It has been said that the principles of English gardening were undoubtedly first laid down by English writers, but whether or not this "discovery" of nature be laid to the poets, or to the new-found art of water-color painting which was a great aid to the landscape gardener, or to the gardeners, themselves, the fact remains that the return to nature was the great revolution in gardening in the latter part of the 18th century.

Repton occupies a very definite place in the history of gardening and his books occupy an equally definite place in garden literature, a topic of fascinating interest for all time. It was not until he had tried his hands at numerous careers that the idea of finding profit in his love of drawing which had been his greatest source of enjoyment since a boy, seems to have occurred to him. This choice proved most successful and he was consulted alike by the greatest landowner and the smallest proprietor. In his travels about the country he acquired the habit of making notes concerning the improvement of the places he visited and of making maps and sketches of proposed alterations. He was a beautiful draughtsman, and used to make two sets of drawings, one to illustrate the existing effect and the other the suggested modifications. He invented an ingenious slide which consisted of a movable slip of paper which covered the part of the view which the landscape gardener proposed to alter. Any number of slides could be used which made the saving in drawing considerable.

The Haverhill Public Library's monthly bulletin with an article on Humphrey Repton. *Courtesy Virginia Bilmazes Bernard Estate.*

Chapter 4
INTERMEZZO: 1924–26

Myrta Little's marriage to Arthur Davies in April 1923 was not the only change affecting Lovecraft's visits to the Merrimack Valley. Eleven months later, Lovecraft also married. His marriage to fellow amateur journalist Sonia H. Greene occurred on 3 March 1924, and he moved into her apartment in New York City. Finances deteriorated after Sonia lost her lucrative position, preventing all but a handful of trips as Lovecraft struggled with poverty and xenophobia in a city known as a melting pot, while Sonia sought work in the Midwest while suffering health problems.

Myrta Little Davies's only child, Robert Little Davies, was born 24 April 1924, the day before her first anniversary. Her son was born with health issues that required constant supervision. These ailments plagued him until his death in 1953. She became a stay-at-home mother whose sole escape was her prolific writing of innocuous short stories for the McClure Newspaper Syndicate. Her husband left the ministry and became a teacher in the Hampstead school system. Her correspondence with Lovecraft dwindled, and she disappears from references in his letters.

Otherwise, life continued as always among Lovecraft's correspondents. Edgar Davis, who had been sent to summer camp in Maine, sent Lovecraft a letter written on birch bark.[1] Tryout Smith continued to convalesce in Plaistow, and with his press set up in the basement of the house, he returned to monthly releases of the *Tryout*.

Lovecraft's involvement in organized amateur journalism diminished considerably. He was distancing himself, not for lack of interest, but because of the energy-sapping ordeal of petty politics. Holding together squabbling factions within the United Amateur Press Association, which itself had been created by a schism in 1912, was a thankless and onerous task. Starting with the 1920–21 election, Lovecraft had been elected official editor for the UAPA, but he lost the election of 1922–23 to a slate specifically campaigning against his insistence on high literary standards; his faction was then reelected in 1923–24, he as official editor and Sonia as president. The final straw for Lovecraft was the refusal of the outgoing treasurer to turn over organization funds, crippling a group already starting a death spiral. Both membership and funds were dwindling. The officers were reelected in 1924–25 by default—there was no convention and therefore no election. In July 1925, Lovecraft addressed 200 ballots for the 1925–26 election, the remaining voting membership. The 1925–26 election found a new president in Lovecraft's protégé Edgar J. Davis.

Edgar Davis of Merrimac, c. 1929.

Although Lovecraft hoped that Davis and his designated official editor Victor E. Bacon could revive the group, he was not optimistic. Tryout Smith suggested that perhaps it was time to merge the UAPA with the National Amateur Press Association. It was not the first time the suggestion had been made, but as with previous attempts, it was dismissed. In a note to Maurice W. Moe, Lovecraft confided:

> Don't you think there's a half-chance for the United to come back with two such cherubs as its leaders? With Davis's brains, & Bacon's restless egotism and energy to prod those brains into action, we certainly have a team whose possibilities are not to be sneez'd at . . . we may be able to postpone hiring the mortician for a year or two more.[2]

Even if Edgar Davis could have resuscitated the organization, he simply didn't have the time—he had been accepted at Harvard University and had just moved to the Boston suburb of Arlington. Davis graduated Harvard in 1929 with an A.B. and then stayed an additional two years studying law. Davis and Bacon did go down swinging—the faltering group managed to publish several comparatively small issues of their journal during Edgar's tenure.[3] No election was held in 1926, and the book quietly closed on this particular chapter of amateur journalism.

In September 1925, Lovecraft wrote to his friend and fellow writer Clark Ashton Smith in California mentioning that he was enclosing a new story; the idea had come from Tryout Smith, still exiled to Plaistow.[4] Smith's concept was that an undertaker is trapped in the village winter tomb where he is readying the coffins for spring thaw. The undertaker escapes by piling the coffins into a platform and enlarging the transom window over the locked door to escape.

The result was Lovecraft's short story "In the Vault." The story does not mention Plaistow specifically (or any other real geographic location), but Peck Valley could easily be Plaistow. The tale opens in the small village of Peck Valley where the local undertaker takes some shortcuts in furnishing the coffin of his dead, and disliked, neighbor, saving himself some time and money at his enemy's expense. The wind blows shut the door to the tomb, and the undertaker finds himself trapped in the receiving vault among the stored coffins. Faced with freezing to death, he stacks up the coffins to create an impromptu platform so that he can crawl out the transom window. He discovers that his shoddy coffin construction practices and questionable embalming methods can provoke some post-mortem retaliation.

Lovecraft submitted "In the Vault" to *Weird Tales,* but it was rejected in November. In an unpublished letter to his aunt Lillian Clark, Lovecraft reported that editor Farnsworth Wright was being cautious about gruesome tales after an uproar following publication of the necrophilia-themed story by C. M. Eddy, Jr., "The Loved Dead."[5] "In the Vault" appeared, appropriately enough, in the November 1925 issue of the *Tryout,* with a dedication to C. W. Smith. It would be the last potentially salable story he would offer Tryout Smith, although the stream of brief essays and poetry continued unabated.

Tryout's inspiration for the story remains a mystery. There is no receiving vault in Plaistow, and there never has been. The town was so small that if there was a winter death that could not be interred immediately, the funeral home itself handled storage until spring thaw. So, although Tryout was living in Plaistow, a Plaistow graveyard was not the inspiration for the story. Of the three cemeteries in Haverhill most familiar to Tryout, none appear to have a winter vault similar enough to the one in Peck Valley to be the spark of the story.[6] The best this author can offer is that 1924 had been the fiftieth anniversary of the completion of Lincoln's tomb at Oak Ridge Cemetery in Springfield, Illinois, and a postcard of the receiving vault, where the body was stored while the memorial was being constructed, was re-released as "Lincoln's original tomb." It shows a vault in the side of a hill with a metal door and a small transom window. Between Lovecraft's letter writing prolificacy, Sonia's employments in the Midwest, and the various correspondents of Tryout himself, it seems reasonable to assume that a copy of the Lincoln tomb postcard would eventually arrive at Groveland Street, if only as a potential addition to Tryout's stamp collection.

Tryout Smith took his stamp collecting seriously. A letter by Lovecraft to James Morton in 1924 discusses the "Ardinii Varini" stamp and reminds Morton to send such stamps to Tryout.[7] The letter contains as much discussion of the stamp as it does the other big news Lovecraft had to share—his recent marriage.

Edgar's sister Ada may also have a connection to Lovecraft through Tryout's inspiration. The name of the old village doctor in "In the Vault" was Davis. Lovecraft wrote the story in September 1925 at the same time that Ada started classes at Boston University Medical School. Dr. A. Frances Davis opened her practice in the family house in Merrimac, where it remained until 1966, when she retired and turned to missionary work. She died in 1991 and lies in the family plot in Plaistow.[8]

Although his visits to the Merrimack Valley had not produced any stories, the town remained in Lovecraft's thoughts in New York City.

In December, he wrote a letter to Lillian Clark noting that he had just tried unsuccessfully to borrow the new book on Timothy Dexter by Newburyport resident John P. Marquand.[9] If this is not ample evidence of his nostalgia for his previous trips to the area, note the Christmas quatrain Lovecraft sent to Edgar Davis at the end of 1925; in four lines Lovecraft combined Edgar's college, Timothy Dexter's booklet title, Tryout, and the Merrimack River.

> May Santa bring to Harvard's brightest son
> A Pickle for a Very Knowing One,
> Whilst Father Charles and reed-crown'd Merrimack
> Unite to swell with praise his gen'rous pack.[10]

Belying the generally even tone of his letters, Lovecraft was emotionally exhausted and depressed. His marriage was faltering because of the long-distance relationship with Sonia, and his distaste of New York was growing. Lovecraft's aunts finally suggested that he come home to Rhode Island. In the spring of 1926, Lovecraft returned to Providence and, restored by his beloved city, his spirits soon lifted. Lovecraft's

Illustrated label from John P. Marquand's first major book. The image of Dexter and his dog is based on an 1805 engraved portrait by James Akin.

September ended on a high note. His creativity no longer stifled, he soon wrote "The Call of Cthulhu," then "Pickman's Model." Although "Pickman's Model" is set in Boston, the ancient tunnels in the North End strongly resemble those in Newburyport running under the main streets to the harbor, a mystery widely published and one that Lovecraft could not have overlooked.[11]

As the month ended, he received additional good news. Tryout Smith was feeling like his old self, and he was returning to Haverhill. The decision may not have been entirely his own. Soon after Tryout moved back to Groveland Street, his son-in-law sold the Plaistow property.

At the end of July, Lovecraft began corresponding with August Derleth, a colleague whose long-term impact on Lovecraft is undeniable, as both his advocate and as cofounder of Arkham House. In 1926, the young fan was just beginning his own career as a writer. In November, Lovecraft again demonstrates his fondness for Tryout Smith by encouraging Derleth to send material for the *Tryout* to publish. Well aware of Smith's typographical challenges, Lovecraft notes an agreement with Tryout whereby Lovecraft was allowed to proofread all submittals to the *Tryout* that he had arranged. Derleth immediately sent four pieces to the journal.[12]

As the old publisher settled back in on Groveland Street, he received a swift submittal from Lovecraft for the next *Tryout*. "The Return" is a 32-line pastoral celebrating Smith's return to Haverhill.[13] In truth, Lovecraft's verse on the joyous return to a familiar and beloved location could just as easily be autobiographical. If there was any doubt as to that double meaning, it should be removed by that year's Christmas quatrain sonnet to Tryout:

> Restor'd to ancient scenes where I belong,
> Returning gladness fills my annual song;
> And doubly glad I am when I address
> Tryout, rejoicing in like happiness![14]

Chapter 5
INNSMOUTH ASCENDANT: 1927–31

In January 1927, Lovecraft began work on a new novel, *The Case of Charles Dexter Ward*. He finished it in March, but it would not see publication until an abridged version ran in *Weird Tales* in 1941. The titular figure is a resident of Providence who discovers he is a direct descendant of Joseph Curwen, to whom he bears a striking physical resemblance. Curwen is a notorious colonial figure rumored to have practiced the dark arts. Ward soon is recreating Curwen's work, and ultimately he resurrects his colonial ancestor. When Ward's behavior seems to change, his family doctor soon realizes that Curwen somehow has taken Ward's place.

A recurring theme in the story is the scent of old buildings as a precursor and olfactory warning of proximity to evil. Lovecraft uses a variety of nouns and adjectives to foreshadow and describe events. The terms range from *scent, smell,* and *odor* to *foetor, stench, malodorous,* and *mephitic,* but all seem rooted in a concept that Lovecraft had about old structures. After a visit to the Paul Revere house in Boston with Edith Miniter in 1923, Lovecraft wrote to Galpin that he felt that the "odour of them alone is sufficient to awake dark speculation." And the most pronounced location of this sinister allurement to Lovecraft was the "antient Ward house in Haverhill, the oldest part of which was built in 1640."[1]

The personal names in *The Case of Charles Dexter Ward* seem to derive from Lovecraft's travels. The story takes place in Lovecraft's beloved Providence, but the name of the family doctor is Marinus Willett, a name that appears in three cemeteries in New York City that Lovecraft may have encountered in his wanderings, two in Manhattan and one in Brooklyn. More telling is the character of Charles Dexter Ward, whose name could be a composite of names Lovecraft encountered during a trip to the Merrimack Valley. Specifically Charles (W. "Tryout" Smith) + (Timothy) Dexter + (John) Ward.

Hypothetical naming patterns aside, Lovecraft's next trip to the Merrimack Valley would have to wait until August. He made up for lost time with a two-week whirlwind tour with stops in Maine, Vermont, New Hampshire, and Massachusetts. He arrived in Portsmouth, a town that rivaled Newburyport as a favorite destination, on Sunday the 28th, eight days into the trip.

> The two towns are probably the most ancient-looking places of large size in America. Both have networks of narrow unpaved sidewalks in the poorer sections—just as they were before the Revolution, same houses and all.[2]

On a postcard to Donald Wandrei sent from Newburyport, Lovecraft makes a similar observation about neighborhoods of unpaved roads and sidewalk-free colonial houses of Portsmouth and Newburyport. Instead of "poorer sections," he bluntly declared the neighborhoods slums.[3] The description may not be charitable, but it demonstrates a dichotomy in Lovecraft's perception of the towns. That dichotomy would eventually allow him to mentally separate sections of the town into entirely different villages, which would prove useful in future writings.

He departed Portsmouth and arrived in Newburyport on Monday, 29 August, and stayed two days, boarding overnight at the YMCA on State Street. On Tuesday, he took a side trip to the Parker River and climbed a hill to get "one of the finest views in New England."[4] Tuesday afternoon, he took the trolley to Amesbury and transferred to Haverhill.

As was his preference, Lovecraft stayed at the YMCA. The YMCA at that time was at 75 Main Street. The location today is a nondescript parking lot behind City Hall at the corner of Main and Summer streets, but in its day it boasted a 45-foot-long swimming pool, a gymnasium, and a reading room with an open fireplace, benefits of operating the facilities in the former home of Haverhill industry mogul and philanthropist E. J. M. Hale. The YMCA moved in 1951 to its current location on Winter Street. Today, all that remains of the elegant Second Empire home are the granite gateposts that mark the entrances to Lovecraft's budget-conscious choice in lodging.

The original entrance to the Newburyport Public Library.

Lovecraft compared the various YMCAs he had stayed during this last trip, assessing them as if he were a transient lodging aficionado. He considered the Portland YMCA "immaculate, artistic and magnificent" but panned the Haverhill YMCA, calling it "rotten" because the amenities were scattered across the estate's various buildings. Newburyport's Y did not fare much better. Lovecraft described it as "seedy and run-down."[5]

His opinion notwithstanding, Lovecraft checked in at the YMCA on Main Street and proceeded down to Groveland Street for a visit with Tryout Smith. Smith, always seeking content for *Tryout,* apparently insisted that HPL write up his trip as a travelogue, with the first part of "The Trip of Theobald" written on the spot.[6] On Wednesday the 31st, Lovecraft returned to Newburyport by trolley through Groveland and West Newbury. There, he took another brief look around Newburyport, walking from the Market Square trolley stop to the train station on Winter Street at Pleasant. Any of the major streets would offer ample architecture for sightseeing. He continued on to Ipswich by train, where he explored the towns of Essex, Gloucester, Magnolia, Manchester, and Salem, and still managed to return to Providence by midnight of Friday, 2 September. Over the next eight years, he would take at least two antiquarian trips, one in the spring and one in the summer, exploring increasingly wider areas at a similarly breakneck pace.

The purpose of these jaunts was in part to explore old bookstores.

Lovecraft collected the *Old Farmer's Almanack* and was always looking for issues. In October 1927, he wrote to Walter J. Coates that he possessed issues continuously back to 1839, with scattered issues to 1805. His goal was a complete set beginning with the first issue of 1773.[7] With the topic of the letter coming so soon after his travels, it suggests Lovecraft may have acquired another edition this trip.

In 1928, Lovecraft embarked on another whirlwind tour. Sonia had returned to New York City, and Lovecraft went there to help his wife set up a hat shop business in Brooklyn. By June he had fled the city, visiting the Hudson Valley, Vermont, and central Massachusetts. The visit to Athol and Wilbraham in central Massachusetts gave rise to his next story, "The Dunwich Horror," steeped with folklore and images acquired during the visit. The story was published in the April 1929 issue of *Weird Tales*. Debate continues as to whether Lovecraft's reference to a rock-strewn hill with a sacrificial altar derives from a visit to North Salem, New Hampshire, home to America's Stonehenge, then known as Pattee's Caves.[8]

Monument to Hannah Duston, now located in GAR Park. *Courtesy of Scott T. Goudsward.*

Lovecraft did not return to the Merrimack Valley until October 1931. In the meantime, his marriage ended,[9] and he visited Cape Cod, ventured south as far as Key West, and toured Quebec. Lovecraft's letter to the editor of the *Providence Sunday Journal* of 20 March 1929 argued against demolition of a row of brick warehouses built in 1815. Lovecraft compared their ability to evoke the city's historical past as being similar to the way Newburyport or Newport uses its historic structures instead of demolishing them.[10] The attempt was futile, but it showed that the Merrimack Valley remained in Lovecraft's mind.

Even while traveling in Quebec in 1930, Lovecraft found a connection back to Haverhill. Upon returning to Providence, he undertook his single longest literary work—*A Description of the Town of Quebeck, in New-France, Lately added to His Britannick Majesty's Dominions.*[11] The section covering King William's War recounts the story of Haverhill's axe-toting colonial folk-figure Hannah Duston.

Duston was captured in 1697 by an Abenaki war party. The natives killed her newborn infant and, after fifteen days of hard travel, Duston and two companions found themselves exchanged to another group of Abenaki to bring the captives north to Canada and into French slavery. Camped on an island in the Merrimack River, Duston killed the Indians while they slept and scuttled all but one of the canoes and headed down river. Almost immediately, she turned the canoe around and scalped the ten corpses for proof of her heroism. Once safely home, Hannah's husband decided that even though the bounty on Indian scalps had been revoked, her wife should get the bounty anyway. The legislature agreed, and Hannah Duston became a *cause célèbre* for killing and mutilating a group of Indians.

Lovecraft notes that she was the "prime heroine of her region" and that Haverhill honored her with a "sumptuous monument in the main square." That main square was a small green where Summer Street, Main Street, and Vestry Place met. Today, after urban renewal, Vestry Place is gone and Winter Street has been straightened to meet Summer Street at Main Street, necessitating the relocating of another statue to nearby GAR Park.

Lovecraft made the trip in October with W. Paul Cook. Both men were at low points in their careers. Cook, still struggling to regain his equilibrium after the death of his wife in 1930, had finally settled in at a new job in Boston in September 1931. Lovecraft's confidence had been shattered by recent rejections. *Weird Tales* had passed on *At the Mountains of Madness.* G. P. Putnam's Sons had asked to see some of his work for a possible book, but the project fell through in mid-July. As bad as the rejections had been, adding insult to the injury, Putnam had handled his manuscripts so badly that they were all but unusable for future submittals. Derleth offered to retype "In the Vault," a story that had become and would remain among his favorites. He urged Lovecraft to resubmit the story to *Weird Tales*. Lovecraft was reticent to do so, but felt obligated after Derleth had retyped the manuscript. He warned Derleth of the likely outcome of rejection, mailed the manuscript to the publisher, and headed out on his trip with Cook.[12]

The trip was an unexpected alignment of opportunities—unseasonably warm weather and Cook feeling well enough to explore (and he had an automobile). Lovecraft used the opportunity to introduce Cook to Newburyport, a town he still referred to as "about as quaint & ancient as any town I've ever seen."[13] As usual, a visit to Newburyport included a side trip to Haverhill and Tryout Smith. Donald Wandrei received a postcard of Haverhill's Kenoza Lake postmarked October 4 from Haverhill, marking the Haverhill trip:

> Amateur conclave at Haverhill—Tryout & Recluse meet for the first time in person with Grandpa as a benign spectator. Yesterday WPC & I saw the south shore, with Hingham's Old Ship Church (1681), & now we're going to ancient Newburyport.[14]

Cook apparently agreed with Lovecraft's assessment—with the warm weather holding, the two returned for another visit in late October, starting in Portsmouth and heading first to Newburyport, then to Salem and Marblehead.[15] Newburyport would prove to be the inspiration needed to rouse Lovecraft's muse. Upon arriving back in Providence, he began work on "The Shadow over Innsmouth." The story, after several false starts, was written in November and December 1931.

The story opens with raids on the wretched colonial seaport of Innsmouth in February 1928. The federal government arrested many residents and dynamited a number of buildings, and there were even rumors that Navy submarines had fired torpedoes at Devil's Reef off the coast. The man who instigated the investigation was an Ohio genealogist named Robert Olmstead.[16] Olmstead was exploring the northeast tracing his New England family lines. Having finished his genealogical research in Newburyport, he planned to proceed to Arkham by train.

He balks at the price of the ticket, and the ticket agent, who is not a native and therefore not completely cognizant of what he is suggesting, offers an alternative. Olmstead could take a bus to Arkham, but is warned that the bus makes a stop in Innsmouth first. The ticket agent at the B&M train station in Newburyport at the time was Arthur C. Holland, whose parents were from Canada, making him the real-life version of a non-local ticket agent.[17]

The agent explains that Innsmouthians are an unpleasantly odd lot and Newburyport folks instinctively dislike the town and its denizens. Olmstead is intrigued that any town could instill such loathing and decides to explore it by taking the 10 AM bus to Innsmouth and then the 8 PM bus to Arkham. He spends the rest of the day in Newburyport researching the village, but he finds little information about the town, as if its very existence is being deliberately covered up (much as Charles Dexter Ward found Joseph Curwen's existence had been virtually expunged from the public record).

The next day, Olmstead takes the bus to Innsmouth and discovers that what was once a vibrant fishing village is now the epitome of decay, not only in the appearance of the people and structures but also in its very essence. When he finally is about to leave the town, he encounters an elderly local who knows its history. Plying him with alcohol, Olmstead is told a bizarre story of the unholy dealings of a local sea captain with amphibian creatures, the "deep ones," who now dwell at the bottom of a low-lying reef off the coast, trading gold for human sacrifice. It seems the creatures also mate with humans. As the hybrid offspring age, their human nature is supplanted by the ichthyic and the amphibian, giving rise to the distinctive and repulsive "Innsmouth look." Fearing that he has been seen indiscreetly learning the town's secrets, Olmstead attempts to leave, only to discover the bus to Arkham has "broken down" and cannot be fixed before morning. With growing trepidation, Olmstead checks in at the decrepit hotel, but finds no safety there. Climbing out the window, Olmstead flees into the night, barely escaping the hordes of giant fish-frog hybrids in hot pursuit. Even once safely back in Ohio after the government raids, Innsmouth haunts Olmstead.

Postcard of the entry to the Newburyport Library from the time of Lovecraft's visits. *Courtesy of the Newburyport Archival Center at the Newburyport Public Library.*

The section of the story that takes place in Newburyport is the culmination of Lovecraft's visits there, with added elements filtered from visits to Haverhill. Similarly, Devil's Reef was drawn from his glass-bottomed boat tour of coral reefs in Biscayne Bay during his trip to Miami in June. Olmstead stays at the YMCA, as Lovecraft often did. Located next to the Newburyport Public Library, it would be a convenient site for an antiquarian such as Lovecraft or Olmstead. The librarian gives Olmstead a note of introduction to the Newburyport Historical Society; it allows him access to the museum, even though it is closed that day. Access to the closed historical society echoes Lovecraft's visit to Haverhill in 1921, when he toured the Historical Society thanks to Myrta Little's intervention with curator Leonard Woodman Smith.

The name of curator Anna Tilton may resonate with Newburyport historians, though not for association with the museum. At the time of Lovecraft's first visit to Newburyport, the superintendent of the public library's reading room was Miss Helen E. Tilton (1861–1930), who lived less than 500 feet from the Historical Society building. Basically, Lovecraft met a real Miss Tilton who lived near the historical society and worked at the library and turned her into a fictional Miss Tilton who lived near the library and worked at the Historical Society.

The Newburyport YMCA where Lovecraft stayed.

While at the historical society (the actual name is The Historical Society of Old Newbury), Olmstead sees a piece of rare gold jewelry from Innsmouth, unnaturally delicate and mesmerizing. The real museum obviously does not own Innsmouth gold, but it does have "The Landlocked Lady," a ship's figurehead that never actually went to sea. Carved with a flowing robe and decorated with painted gold jewelry, she is a reminder of the rich shipbuilding industry in Newburyport. Philip Shreffler, in *The H. P. Lovecraft Companion* (1977), somewhat optimistically suggests that the gold-painted ornamentation on the figurehead was the inspiration of the description of the Innsmouth jewelry.[18]

The next morning, Olmstead waits for the bus at Market Square in front of Hammond's Drug Store. As the arrival time for the bus draws near, the square begins to empty out, people wandering off or stepping into the Ideal Lunch to avoid contact with any passengers for Innsmouth. Again Lovecraft is using local landmarks—the local Ideal Lunch franchise was in Newburyport's Market Square (5 State Street) and also served as the ticket agent for the B&M bus lines. It is across State Street from Charles Perry's Drug Store. Why Lovecraft would identify the Ideal Lunch room by name but not Perry's Drugstore is a mystery, but it is interesting to note that the buses in Haverhill stopped in Washington Square, in front of Gammon's Drug Store, located in the Coombs building at the corner of Washington Square and Essex Street.

Lovecraft carefully differentiates between Innsmouth and Newburyport, both in the story and in his correspondence. He specifically notes that the bus route proceeds along High Street, passing landmarks in neighboring Newbury before reaching a long stretch of open shoreline before leaving the main highway to Rowley and Ipswich (Route 1A). Finally losing sight of Plum Island, the bus crests a hill from where Olmstead can see the entire Manuxet River valley. This route description may offer the only clue to a reference in "The Trip of Theobald" travelogue. In that article, published in the September 1927 issue of the *Tryout*, Lovecraft mentions that he made a "side trip to Parker River" and climbing a hill to get "one of the finest views in New England." When, in "The Shadow over Innsmouth," Olmstead is on the Innsmouth bus, the landmarks he notes, the Lower Green and Parker River, indicate that they have left Newburyport and are now in Newbury. Both landmarks are at the base of "Old Town Hill."[19] The 168-foot coastal promontory still offers a panoramic view from the summit as far as the Isles of Shoals and Mount Agamenticus in southern Maine.

View looking over the marsh grass to Plum Island.

Using the travel descriptions in "The Shadow over Innsmouth" itself, we can see that Innsmouth is actually about 15 miles south of Newburyport along the coast. Lovecraft places the town south of Plum Island but north of Cape Ann, with Ipswich and Rowley nearby. This would roughly place Innsmouth in the tidal marshes of Essex, Massachusetts, at the mouth of the Essex River.[20] This is where Lovecraft's ability to distill Newburyport down into the parts he liked and the parts he disliked becomes evident.

There is no question that Newburyport inspired Innsmouth; Lovecraft himself states as much in letters to such correspondents as August Derleth, Fritz Leiber, and Robert Bloch.[21] The parts of Newburyport that Lovecraft appreciated became the idealized Newburyport of the story—an antiquarian's dream, with the beautifully maintained buildings and amply stocked research facilities. Innsmouth was a composite of the areas of Newburyport Lovecraft considered blights upon the city, drawing on his first impressions from the trip to the town in 1923 with Edgar Davis from the trolley along the Merrimack River. Newburyport is epitomized by the library, the historical society, and High Street. Innsmouth is represented by abandoned shipyards and rotted docks along the Merrimack and ramshackle clam digger huts of Joppa Flats.

In November 1931, writing to Clark Aston Smith after a series of rejections, Lovecraft expressed doubt in his writing ability and nearly convinced himself it may be time to stop altogether. He tells Smith that the story he is working on is an experiment in which he is trying different moods and tempos.

> What I shall—or shan't—write hereafter depends to some extent on how I come out with these experiments. My latest move is to destroy all three versions written to date, preparatory to embarking on a fourth. The trouble with most of my stuff is that it falls between two stools—the vile magazine type subconsciously engrafted on my method by W[eird] T[ales] association, and the real story. My tales are not bad enough for cheap editors, nor good enough for standard acceptance and recognition.[22]

He expressed similar discouragement in a letter to Derleth, who convinced Lovecraft to reconsider "The Shadow over Innsmouth" and to look at the handwritten manuscript one last time so see if there was a chance the story could be salvaged.[23] "The Shadow over Innsmouth" would become one of Lovecraft's most popular stories, but he would not find a magazine willing to buy the story in his lifetime.

Fortunately, 1932 was a better year for Lovecraft; obviously he continued to write. Newburyport would remain a favorite travel destination. He would return in 1932 with W. Paul Cook for a more celestial form of sightseeing.

The Newburyport B&M Railroad Station.

Gammon's Drug Store, Coombs Building, Haverhill (photo c. 1931). *Courtesy of the Trustees of the Haverhill Public Library, Special Collections Department.*

Tryout Smith and W. Paul Cook. *Courtesy John Hay Library, Brown University.*

Chapter 6
DREAMS AND ECLIPSES: 1932–33

The year 1931 may have closed with Lovecraft having grave doubts about his writing, but 1932 began with a kind of byline for him. In January, Tryout Smith published *Thoughts and Pictures*, a collection of poems by amateur journalist and poet Rev. Eugene B. Kuntz. Lovecraft, who wrote the two-page foreword on Kuntz's poetry, probably revised the 22-page booklet as well. As noted on the cover, the booklet was "Co-operatively Published by H. P. Loveracft [*sic*] and C. W. Smith." The "tryoutism" continued to prevail.

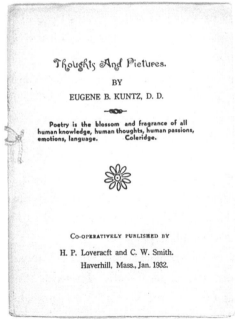

A collection of poems, edited (and probably revised) by Lovecraft and published by Tryout Smith in 1932. Note the ever-present tryoutism on the cover.

And then in February, Lovecraft undertook "The Dreams in the Witch House." His work with Tryout was still fresh in his mind. The story takes place in the "legend-haunted city of Arkham," but the protagonist, Walter Gilman, a student at Miskatonic University, hails from Haverhill. Gilman is a common surname in Haverhill.

Gilman is studying mathematics and folklore at Miskatonic. He has come to Miskatonic specifically to study "non-Euclidean calculus and quantum physics," an unusual double major, because he believes they are related to legends of magic in folklore. Gilman's studies uncover the legend of Keziah Mason, who lived in Arkham in the late seventeenth century. Mason, who was arrested as a witch during the Salem witch trials, mysteriously escaped from the Salem jail, leaving behind an insane jailer and a perplexed Cotton Mather who puzzled over angles and lines smeared on the wall of the cell. Gilman is fascinated by the witch's trial, where she claimed to Judge Hathorne that lines and curves could be made to point out directions leading through the walls of space to other spaces beyond. This talk from a supposedly illiterate colonial hag intrigues Gilman because it appears to be a simplified version of his own theories.

He discovers that the building where Keziah Mason dwelt in Arkham still stands. To inspire his research into the Keziah Mason case, he ill-advisedly moves into the oddly angled garret where the witch once dwelled. Whether caused by the room, his consultation of the university library's dreaded tomes, or overwork, Gilman starts suffering nightmares. His dreams are plagued by visions of aliens and witches. He begins to dream that he is traveling through dimensions and comes to realize Keziah Mason was intuitively able to use interspatial geometry to travel through hyperspace.

After a baby from Arkham is kidnapped, Gilman dreams that he stops Keziah from sacrificing a baby. The next morning, Gilman is found dead in his room in the Witch House, a grisly reminder of the danger of exploring secrets best left alone.

Unsure of his abilities and of the story's merit, Lovecraft sent the manuscript among his friends for opinions. Reaction ranged from favorable (Clark Ashton Smith and Donald Wandrei) to tepid (Bernard Dwyer). Then, the manuscript reached August Derleth. Derleth thought the story was poor by Lovecraft's standards, but exactly what the pulps were looking for. For Lovecraft, who had been lambasting the lack of quality of pulps, this was the story's death knell.[1]

By this time, Lovecraft had learned that "In the Vault" had been accepted by *Weird Tales,* proving that Derleth's insistence about resubmitting it had been correct. If Derleth was right about "In the Vault," there was no reason to doubt his instincts about "The Dreams in the Witch House." Lovecraft wrote back to Derleth, noting that he expected criticism, but "hardly thought the miserable mess was quite as bad as you found it . . ." He concluded that "The whole incident shows me that my fictional days are probably over."[2] Lovecraft put "Witch House" aside and moved on.

"In the Vault" appeared in the April 1932 issue of *Weird Tales,* where it found itself in good company. Other stories in the issue included tales from Lovecraft's friends Henry S. Whitehead and Clark Ashton Smith and a reprint of "Berenice" by Edgar Allan Poe.

The story proved to be popular among both the *Weird Tales* readership and Lovecraft's circle. Clark Ashton Smith thought that "Your 'In the Vault' certainly stands out in the current WT." Robert E. Howard, another of Lovecraft's correspondents (best remembered for creating Conan the Barbarian), offered similar sentiments: "Your latest story in Weird Tales is as grim and gripping a tale as I ever read."[3]

An extensive travel itinerary found Lovecraft exploring the southern states to New Orleans and back, hopping across the region. The extensive return trip was cut short by news that his elderly aunt Lillian Clark had fallen gravely ill. He rushed back to Providence, arriving on July 1 to find her hospitalized and in a comatose state. She died 3 July 1932.

After his grief subsided somewhat, Lovecraft began planning a return visit to Quebec. But before that adventure, there was room for a trip to Newburyport. On 30 August, Lovecraft met Cook in Boston. The next day, they headed to Newburyport to view the solar eclipse.

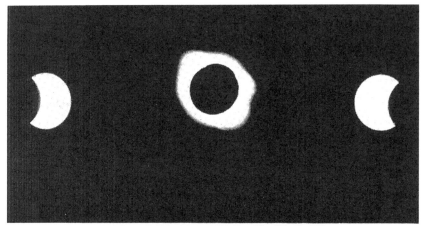

THE ECLIPSE OF THE SUN—PORTLAND, ME., AUG. 31, 1932

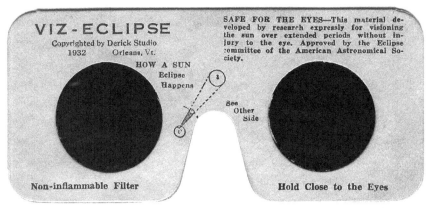

The 1932 solar eclipse was a social event that produced hotel specials, eclipse cruises, and a cottage industry of filters, viewers, and postcards. *Viz-Eclipse glasses courtesy of Peter Bealo, Plaistow, NH.*

Lovecraft had been fascinated by astronomy from an early age; his first published work (other than letters to editors) was a series of astronomy articles in the *Pawtuxet Valley Gleaner* in 1906.[4] When he learned that a total eclipse would be visible in parts of Massachusetts, New Hampshire, and Maine, he did not hesitate. He knew the crowds would flock to the line of maximum duration in New Hampshire and Maine, but he was content to avoid the masses and to see his second eclipse by choosing a slightly shorter duration.

It really matters relatively little whether an amateur sees the totality for half a minute, or for a minute & a half, so long as he does see it. Even a momentary flash gives the full benefit of the corona. In 1925 (when I was in New York) some of us tramped up into the cold of northern Yonkers to see the January eclipse, but [Frank Belknap] Long (judging from his description) seems to have seen about as much from the roof of his apartment house in 100th St."[5]

Cook and Lovecraft stopped for a brief visit at Groveland Street. Tryout Smith was, as always, invited to accompany them. As usual, Smith declined, planning to see the eclipse from Haverhill, where it would last only two seconds or so.

Lovecraft and Cook arrived in Newburyport on 31 August. Lovecraft's previous explorations of Newburyport clued him as to the ideal spot at which to witness the eclipse—the open spaces of Atkinson Common. This landmark, between Merrimack and High streets in the northern part of town, was founded in 1873 and consisted of winding paths along 21 acres of landscaped lawns around a lily pond.

At 3:22 PM, Lovecraft and Cook witnessed the beginning of the rare total eclipse of the sun. His description in a letter to James F. Morton on 3 September was not astronomically precise, but it was pure Lovecraft:

> The aspect of the landskip did not change in tone until the solar crescent was rather small, and then a kind of sunset vividness became apparent. When the crescent waned to extreme thinness, the scene grew strange and spectral—an almost deathlike quality inhering in the sickly yellowish light. Just about that time the sun went under a cloud, and our expedition commenced cursing in 33-1/3 different languages including Ido. At last, though, the thin thread of the pre-totality glitter emerged into a large patch of absolutely clear sky. The outspread valleys faded into unnatural night—Jupiter came out in the deep-violet heavens—ghoulish shadow-bands raced along the winding white clouds—the last beaded strip of glitter vanished—and the pale corona flicker'd into aureolar radiance around the black disc of the obscuring moon.[6]

Lovecraft was not alone in his belief of the Common being an ideal location for sightseeing: several years after his visit, an observation tower was erected in the park.

Lovecraft's letter to Morton refers to Newburyport by name and as "Bossy Gillis's burg." This reference notes how deeply Lovecraft had absorbed local Newburyport atmosphere. Bossy Gillis was Newburyport's most colorful character besides Timothy Dexter. Andrew Jackson "Bossy" Gillis was mayor in 1932, during one of his six non-concurrent terms as mayor between 1928 and 1965. (He also lost the mayoral election twelve more times.) By 1932, Gillis's exploits were being nationally followed. He is best remembered today for his filling station in Market Square, which served as his mayoral office.[7]

The year 1932 ended on a high note. Lovecraft was informed that both "The Strange High House in the Mist" and "In the Vault" warranted mentions by the O. Henry awards, an annual award celebrating short stories of exceptional merit.[8]

As 1933 began, August Derleth asked to see "The Dreams in the Witch House" again,[9] ostensibly to type a file copy of the manuscript; but Derleth had ulterior motives. Unbeknown to Lovecraft, he submitted the story to *Weird Tales*. Derleth may have done so because he knew the sale would help his friend, whose income always was meager. The story's immediate acceptance provided one of the few highlights of 1933.[10]

"The Dreams in the Witch House" appeared in the July 1933 issue of *Weird Tales*. Lovecraft was delighted, but still concerned about the response to the story. He carefully distanced himself from the story's publication by noting that it was Derleth who was responsible for getting the story into print.[11]

In July, Helen V. Sully of Auburn, California, arrived in Providence. Sully had decided to explore the East Coast. Her mother was having an ongoing affair with Clark Ashton Smith, and Smith suggested Helen look up Lovecraft when she reached Providence. Lovecraft set her up at a boarding house across from his home, and the two embarked upon one of Lovecraft's whirlwind tours not only of

Providence, but also of Newport and Newburyport. Sully recalls visiting a graveyard in Newburyport where he explained the various styles of carvings.[12] The cemetery is not named, but the most likely candidates are the Old Hill Burying Ground, founded in 1729, and St. Paul's Episcopal Churchyard, founded in 1711. Both are located off High Street in the middle of town, making them easily accessible by foot. The former is the final resting place of Lovecraft's perennial favorite Newburyporter, Timothy Dexter, and the latter is the first cemetery Lovecraft visited in Newburyport in 1923, in the company of Edgar Davis.

Old Hill Burying Ground.

Helen Sully is better remembered for a different graveyard visit with Lovecraft. In Providence, they visited the graveyard of St. John's Episcopal Cathedral, where Poe once courted Sarah Whitman. Lovecraft frequently brought guests to the graveyard at night. That night, he told a ghost story. The combination of his eerie tone, the darkness, and the grave were too much, and Sully fled the graveyard in tears. When he caught up with her, Sully claimed that he had a strange look of triumph on his face.[13]

After departing Providence, Sully returned to New England for further exploring on her own. Lovecraft's letter to her, dated 27

September, discusses details about a subsequent visit to Newbury-port.[14] He agrees with her assessment of Newburyport after her recent visit and is glad she had time to explore Joppa. He asks if she was able to visit Whittier's birthplace in Haverhill and the Whittier homestead in Amesbury. He adds that he hoped she had time to visit some of the local Newburyport sites, such as the grass-choked waterfront, the "rotting, half-deserted houses south of the Square," and the "old church where George Whitefield is buried."

Whitefield, an English-born Anglican evangelist known for his preaching on both sides of the Atlantic as "the Grand Itinerant," was considered one of the best-known orators in both Britain and the American colonies. Whitefield visited America seven times, but did not survive the final visit. He died in Newburyport and was interred in the basement of the South Church in a crypt directly below the pulpit.

If Lovecraft had visited the church during one of his tours, he would have seen considerably more of Whitefield than Sully. By the time of Helen Sully's return, the crypt had been sealed from

The white headstone of Timothy Dexter in Old Hill Burying Ground stands defiant among a sea of gray slate grave markers. *Courtesy of Allan Sawyer.*

public view after more than a century and half of allowing tourists to view and occasionally handle the skeletal remains of the preacher. Instead, resting on top of the burial alcove is a plaster cast of Whitefield's skull placed atop a plaster replica of his Bible.

Frank Belknap Long, one of Lovecraft's oldest friends, published his recollections of Lovecraft in 1975 and included another graveyard visit misattributed to Newburyport. Long recalls an afternoon with

Lovecraft sitting on the porch of a local resident whose grandparents had been involved in the founding of a spiritualism-oriented religious sect. This led to a discussion of belief in ghosts that culminated in a visit to a fog-shrouded cemetery after dark. Long identifies the visit as taking place in Newburyport, but after forty-five years, Long apparently misremembered the location.[15] There is no record in Lovecraft's published correspondence of him visiting Newburyport with Long. Lovecraft accompanied the Long family to Wareham, Massachusetts, and to the village of Onset.[16] Onset had been developed in the 1880s as a summer camp for spiritualist meetings; it has several local purported ghosts and two cemeteries within walking distance.

As the year ended, Lovecraft's dearth of inspiration persisted. He had seen a few collaborations and revisions published, but he had not published a story of his own since "The Dreams in the Witch House," which had been written the year before. In December, he wrote to Clark Ashton Smith, complaining he could not convert his mental constructs into actual prose on a page.[17] His literary malaise would continue until November 1934, when he began his last major story. It was probably not a coincidence that the story followed one last visit to the Merrimack Valley.

Gravestone of Nathanael Peaslee Junr. *Courtesy of the Trustees of the Haverhill Public Library, Special Collections Department.*

Chapter 7
SHADOWS OUT OF HAVERHILL: 1934–36

Lawrence, Massachusetts, was the scene of a brief and unplanned visit from Lovecraft and W. Paul Cook in 1934. The two had taken the railroad from Boston to Lawrence on 24 August. There, they transferred from the train to the trolley running into Haverhill for a visit with Tryout Smith. Upon arriving in Haverhill, Lovecraft discovered he had left his battered black valise on the trolley. In it were illustrations of one of his stories from *Weird Tales,* earmarked to be sent to R. H. Barlow in Florida. Lovecraft broke the news to Barlow on a postcard of Whittier's Birthplace, on which Cook and Smith also jotted greetings.

Lawrence trolley barn, where in August 1934 Lovecraft and W. Paul Cook retrieved Lovecraft's lost valise. *Courtesy of Special Collections, Lawrence Public Library.*

After the visit, Cook and Lovecraft took the trolley back to Lawrence, learning that lost and found items were stored at the office in trolley car barn on Merrimack Street in Lawrence. The valise was found and Lovecraft scribbled a quick update that the art had been recovered, then dropped the card in the mail as they walked to the train station a little farther up Merrimack Street.[1] The train station, now part of the Senator Patricia McGovern Transportation Center, is one block to the east of the location of the station it replaced in 2005.

This trip to Haverhill apparently included a visit to the Pentucket Burying Ground on Water Street. This detail does not appear in Lovecraft's letters but is hinted at in the story he soon wrote shortly thereafter, "The Shadow out of Time." The story opens with the narrator, Nathaniel Wingate Peaslee of Arkham, Massachusetts, acknowledging that the words he is about to write will be hard to believe. Peaslee was born in his family's ancestral home on Haverhill's Golden Hill along Boardman Street. He is the son of Jonathan and Hannah (Wingate) Peaslee, both of old colonial Haverhill stock. A child of sturdy Yankee roots, Peaslee was raised in Haverhill until becoming an instructor in political economy at Miskatonic University in 1895. He married his hometown sweetheart Alice Keezar the following year. By 1902, Peaslee was a full professor at Miskatonic, with three children: Robert, Wingate, and Hannah.

On Thursday, 14 May 1908, Professor Peaslee had a nervous break-

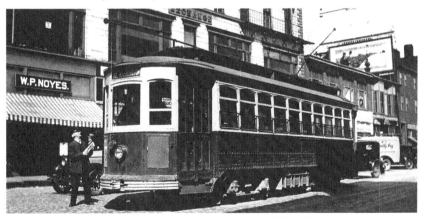

Trolley preparing to depart from a transfer point on Water Street at Main Street in Haverhill in April 1936. *Courtesy of the Trustees of the Haverhill Public Library, Special Collections Department.*

down while teaching a class. When he awoke, he had lost all motor function and literally had to relearn how to talk and to move. His personality and speech patterns changed completely, and his intellect bordered on the preternatural. He began to visit libraries in search of esoteric tomes and traveled to mysterious and exotic locations. His friends and family fearfully abandoned him. Only his son Wingate believed the affliction temporary. But on 17 September 1913, Peaslee's real self returned suddenly and unexpected as in mid-sentence, he resumed his lecture of five years before.

Over the next twenty-two years, odd dream fragments begin to crystallize into a narrative, and Peaslee pieces together what he believes to be a vivid delusion concocted by his subconscious during his amnesiac state. With the help of his son, now a psychology professor at Miskatonic, Peaslee publishes an article in the *Journal of the American Psychological Society* about his dreams as a side effect of abnormally long periods of amnesia.

In July 1935, Peaslee receives a letter from West Australia where an explorer had read of his case. He had discovered, in the deserts of the outback, ancient stone blocks identical to those from Peaslee's dreams. Peaslee and his son immediately mount an expedition to Australia. There he discovers that his ailment was not amnesia but something decidedly worse—something triggered by horrific events that happened over one hundred and fifty million years before.

The story was a difficult one for Lovecraft to tell; he wrote and re-wrote the text repeatedly between November 1934 and February 1935. Some of the story's concepts had been nebulous ideas Lovecraft had played with as early as 1930:

> In an ancient buried city a man finds a mouldering prehistoric document *in English and his own handwriting*, telling an incredible tale. Voyage from present to past implied. Possible actualization of this.[2]

The same concept is mentioned to Clark Ashton Smith in a letter from that time. A letter to Smith in 1932 discusses the concept of minds exchanged over time as a way to avoid paradoxes that inevitably arise in writing about time travel.[3] As late as May 1934, Lovecraft shared the concept with R. H. Barlow as an idea still in progress:

> He told me of a plot-idea of his—based on the disapprobation of the inconsistencies of time-travelling as usually written. The tale concerned a man who traveled to prehistoric times and found chiseled upon a rock words in English, *in his own hand.*[4]

The details regarding Haverhill in "The Shadow out of Time" are as accurate as those regarding Newburyport in "The Shadow over Innsmouth." Before Peaslee secured his position at Miskatonic, he lived in his ancestral family home on Boardman Street on Golden Hill. Rising almost 300 feet above the surrounding area, Golden Hill gives an expansive view of the city and the Merrimack River. The walk to the hilltop's scenic vista would be on Boardman Street, as seen on any of Lovecraft's visits with Tryout Smith. The Riverside neighborhood was then the fastest growing section of Haverhill. Trolley lines allowed workers to raise families outside the downtown yet still within reach of the factories. There were still farms and open fields, but incursions were being made: the new Linwood Cemetery was formerly a large parcel of the Boardman farm, a large land grant that had been in the White-Boardman family since the earliest days of the Pentucket colony.

Lovecraft's affinity for colonial houses would have immediately spotted the simple Federal architectural lines of the homestead of the Mears Dairy Farm. Originally built in 1800, the property had been part of the White family farm, a property that once encompassed both sides of Mill Street, the second oldest street in Haverhill. Charles White bequeathed the property to Charles Boardman, the namesake of the road that runs from Mill Street to Water Street and intersects Groveland Street. In Lovecraft's day, the acreage had been reduced considerably, section by section. The only other building that would have attracted Lovecraft's antiquarian eye would be the Richard Hazen garrison house on the corner of Water and Groveland streets. The house was privately owned by that time, but previously had been restored by antique furniture enthusiast Wallace Nutting as one of his chain of furnished house museums.[5]

The Mears farmhouse (1800) on Boardman Street.

The Hazen Garrison House (c. 1720).

The Peaslee stone stands in front of the Saltonstall family monument.
Courtesy of Scott T. Goudsward.

Whether on the 1934 visit or an earlier trip, Lovecraft's affection for antiquities and his interest in the Salem witch trials ensure that he had visited the Pentucket Burial Grounds at least once. Within easy walking distance of Tryout's home, Haverhill's earliest burial ground contains headstones dating to the seventeenth century and an obelisk dedicated to the mortal remains of Major Nathaniel Saltonstall, a member of the Court of Oyer and Terminer, the judges who oversaw the Salem witch trials. After resigning from the court in June 1692, Saltonstall became a prominent critic of the Salem proceedings (specifically the use of "spectral evidence") and was himself accused of witchcraft as the hysteria began to burn itself out.

Names on stones in the cemetery appear in "The Shadow out of Time" encompassing the entire family of the protagonist. The head-stone of Nathaniel Peaslee, Jr. (1707–1730) is a classic example of the Merrimack Valley School of carving, with a distinctive circular face with round eyes, a linear nose, and oblong mouth. Its inscription reads:

> Here lies interd ye precious dust of Mr Nathanael Peaslee Junr ye only & desirable son of Mr Nathl Peaslee who with comfort took his youthful flight from ye promising joys of earthly possessions in hope of a far more exceeding & eternal weight of glory on Sept ye 9 1730 aged 27 years.

The name *Peaslee* may have been selected because of the proximity of the stone to the Saltonstall stone. Myrta Little could have pointed it out on Lovecraft's visit to Haverhill in 1921; her paternal grandmother was a Peaslee, and the graveyard is passed en route to both the Haverhill Historical Society and to Tryout Smith's home. Elsewhere in the cemetery are Ruth Barnard Peaslee (1651–1723) and Abigail Peasley (1728–1729).

Lovecraft could have picked the name Nathaniel Peaslee based on his reading of Henry David Thoreau, whom he considered "refreshing and indispensable." The list of recommended reading was written in September 1936, after the story was completed, but it demonstrates Lovecraft's familiarity with the author. It was drafted as the concluding chapter of a book on speaking and grammar he was revising. It remained unpublished until 1966, when August Derleth printed it

under the title "Suggestions for a Reading Guide."[6] This is not to
suggest that Lovecraft was an advocate of transcendentalism, merely
that he admired the author's craftsmanship. In fact, Lovecraft had no
use for "any form of supernaturalism—religion, spiritualism, transcendentalism, metempsychosis, or immortality."[7]

Thoreau records visiting the Nathaniel Peaslee garrison in East
Haverhill's Rock Village in April 1853 while in Haverhill doing survey
work.[8] Thoreau mentions the story of Hannah Duston in *A Week on
the Concord and Merrimack Rivers* and notes his visit to the Duston
farmhouse cellar hole in 1859.[9]

But Pentucket itself is probably the source, considering the ill-fated
professor's middle name. Moses Wingate (1769–1870) is also in the
burial ground with a headstone visually different from most of the
colonial stones in the cemetery, a tribute to his longevity, having survived his peers and friends from the colonial age by living into the
Victorian. The headstone is topped by an encircled cross above a sheaf
of wheat being cut by a scythe—classic examples of Victorian design
excess. Wingate is also the middle name of George Wingate Chase, the
author of *History of Haverhill, Massachusetts* (1861).

Lovecraft was known to employ a very subtle brand of humor on
occasion in his works.[10] The use of the Athol/Wilbraham background
material in "The Dunwich Horror" is so subtle that "it could have
evoked a twinkle of comprehension in only a very few readers."[11] That
same sort of sly whimsy also occurs in "The Shadow out of Time" in
the character name selections. In the same paragraph where Professor
Peaslee says he had no interest in the supernatural before his bout of
amnesia, Lovecraft mentions the maiden name of Peaslee's wife—
Alice Keezar. Although there is no Alice Keezar buried in Pentucket,
there is a stone marking the burial of "Sarjant John Keyzar." John
Keezar was killed in 1696/7 during the Indian raid that resulted in the
capture of Hannah Duston. Sergeant Keezar is the father of Cobbler
John Keezer, immortalized by Haverhill's beloved native son John
Greenleaf Whittier in his ballad "Cobbler Keezar's Vision" (1861). In
that poem, the cobbler is transported through time in a mystical vision,

paralleling Professor Peaslee's out-of-body experience.

Lovecraft completed the story in February 1935 but had doubts as to its merits. In a letter to E. Hoffmann Price on 14 March, he confesses his concerns:

> By the way, I finished "The Shadow out of Time" last week, but doubt whether it is good enough to type. Somehow or other, it does not seem to embody quite what I want to—and I may tear it up and start all over again.[12]

The story survived, but remained in manuscript form, handwritten in a notebook. Lovecraft was looking for input, so he sent the notebook to Derleth in February 1935. Derleth kept the notebook for more than five months without reading the story, and Lovecraft finally asked for it back.[13] Since he was visiting R. H. Barlow, he had Derleth send the notebook to him in DeLand, Florida.

When it appeared that Barlow was not reading the story either, he bemoaned the fact in a letter to Duane W. Rimel, noting that even with the bad handwriting, if the story had any merit, either one of them should have gotten through it.[14] However, Barlow had been quietly typing up the manuscript as a surprise. Lovecraft was delighted with the 88-page typescript and immediately mailed it out to his circle of readers. Barlow kept the handwritten manuscript for his collection.

In a letter to Derleth, Lovecraft notes the typescript was "accurately typed," perhaps a subtle dig at the five months Derleth had the story and didn't read it, compared to the results of Barlow in two and a half months. However, at the end of October, he admitted that the text had errors that he had to correct on the typescript.[15] A more grievous error was Barlow's paper choice: the heavier stock held up better to the repeated mailings and handling, but it prevented him from making carbon copies. The typescript was the sole copy other than the original notebook.[16]

In October, Donald Wandrei was the current recipient of "The Shadow out of Time" typescript. Lovecraft announced the sale of *At the Mountains of Madness* to *Astounding Stories*, a new market for him.

Wandrei, a regular contributor that magazine, brought "The Shadow out of Time" typescript to the editor at *Astounding* who purchased it immediately.

At the same time, Lovecraft heard from William L. Crawford, who had contacted him in 1933 looking for stories for his planned non-paying horror magazine, *Unusual Stories*. Lovecraft had submitted several stories that ended up running in Crawford's science-fiction themed *Marvel Tales*. Crawford had reprinted Lovecraft's Dunsanian fantasy "Celephaïs" in *Marvel Tales* with enough typos that Lovecraft fussed about it afterward for months: "anything Hill-Billy handles will be tardy & slipshod."[17]

Although he would become well known as the first publisher to specialize in science fiction, William L. Crawford of Everett, Pennsylvania, was best known at this time for failed attempts at various "semi-professional magazines." He had considered publishing *At the Mountains of Madness* or "The Shadow over Innsmouth" as small books, and then the two combined into one book. When *At the Mountains of Madness* was accepted by *Astounding Stories*, there is some indication that Crawford considered sending "The Shadow over Innsmouth" to the magazine as well. Lovecraft did not encourage Crawford, feeling "Innsmouth" was too far removed from the magazine's science fiction audience.[18] If Crawford did submit it to *Astounding Stories*, it was refused and Lovecraft was not informed.

Lovecraft was reeling from "an attack of grippe which had me flat for a week" in February 1936, followed by his aunt Annie Gamwell's attack of grippe that required hospitalization in March.[19] Lovecraft was not using "grippe" as a term for influenza, which would be common parlance for the time, but rather as a generic term to mention illness in the family without mentioning inappropriate specifics such as his aunt's true illness, which was a cancer-related mastectomy. In Lovecraft's case, the "grippe" was probably a digestive tract issue that did not subside until the summer heat.

By March 1936, Crawford and Lovecraft finally settled on publishing "The Shadow over Innsmouth" in book format. Lovecraft had been corresponding with Crawford for some time, and he was not

impressed with Crawford or optimistic about the project. If the
sobriquet "Hill-Billy" is not sufficient to indicate Lovecraft's recollection of the typos in "Celephaïs," his descriptions of Crawford as a
lad with "a certain callow dulness" and "a comic character at best"
who meant well surely suffice.[20]

Things got worse. When *At the Mountains of Madness* appeared
serialized in *Astounding Stories* (February, March, and April), Lovecraft
considered it so badly edited that he feared for the next issue with
"The Shadow out of Time."

In April, Annie Gamwell was out of the hospital and back in the
home she shared with Lovecraft. As she recovered, Lovecraft
struggled to get his correspondence and finances under control. A
letter at the end of April regretfully declines Barlow's invitation to visit
Florida and remarks on the heavy spring flooding.[21] He notes that
Haverhill's downtown was inundated with six to ten feet of water. The
river crested at thirty feet. Had its level risen another foot, it would
have reached Tryout Smith on Groveland Street.

Postcard showing the flood waters subsiding in Haverhill's Washington Square
in the aftermath of the 1936 flood.

The June 1936 issue of *Astounding Stories* contained "The Shadow
out of Time," and Lovecraft's fears were realized. He considered both
stories as printed in *Astounding Stories* to be in such poor shape as to be

considered unpublished. He regarded the printing of the stories as the worst hack job ever perpetrated upon his work, even worse than anything in the *Tryout*, with paragraph breaks altered, excessive punctuation added, and passages omitted. He was so irritated that he started editing a copy of the magazine issue. Because the single typescript had been sent to the magazine and Barlow had the original notebook, Lovecraft's revisions to the printed "Shadow out of Time" were done from memory and thus incomplete.[22]

The worst was yet to come in November with the arrival of Crawford's *The Shadow over Innsmouth*. Even with multiple proof sheets and corrections, Lovecraft was aghast at the final product, noting "34 bad misprints, a lousy format, & shaky, amateurish binding."[23] The book also came with an errata sheet, the first version of which was so badly misprinted as to be useless.[24] Lovecraft, who took his payment in copies, ended up correcting his copies by hand.

The book sold poorly. Four hundred copies of *The Shadow over Innsmouth* were printed by Crawford, but financial restrictions limited him to binding 200 copies as cheaply as possible. The remaining sheets eventually were destroyed. S. T. Joshi dryly notes that between destroyed sheets and lackluster sales there are probably more copies extant with Lovecraft's handwritten corrections than without.[25]

Gateposts marking the entry of the E. J. M. Hale home in Haverhill. *Courtesy of Joan Goudsward.*

Chapter 8
CODA

By January 1937, complaints of the "grippe" appear more prominently and more frequently in Lovecraft's letters. He surely was aware that this ailment was more than a lingering bug, and one must wonder if his mention of symptoms such as swollen feet, constant pain, inability to take solid foods, and abdominal bloating was his way of preparing his friends and correspondents for the *dénouement*.

Howard Phillips Lovecraft died in Providence, Rhode Island on 15 March 1937, at the age of forty-six. A writer to the end, he maintained a "death diary" for his last few days in the hospital in hopes that his observations of experiencing the terminal stages of intestinal cancer would prove useful to the physicians.[1] For a man who did not believe in an afterlife, his writings have nonetheless bestowed upon him a form of immortality.

Lovecraft would have smiled wryly at what must be the greatest tryoutism of all: When C. W. Smith noted Lovecraft's passing in a touching memorial in the pages of the *Tryout* (April 1937), his friend's name was given as "Howard Prescott Lovecraft."

Tryout Smith continued to churn out issues like clockwork. The final issue was August 1944, ending the *Tryout*'s thirty-year run (255 issues). Charles W. "Tryout" Smith died on February 17, 1948, at the age of ninety-five and was buried in Haverhill's Hilldale Cemetery in a family plot. He had been ill for the last four years. Several attempts were made to continue the *Tryout* by other members of the amateur journalism field, but without Smith's indefinable touch and creative typography the new publications failed.

Burial plot of Charles W. Smith's family in Haverhill's Hilldale Cemetery. *Courtesy Donovan Loucks.*

In 1940, Lovecraft's travel companion and fellow amateur W. Paul Cook decided it was time to collect tributes to his old friend. Many had been solicited, but Cook felt none was better than the one from Tryout Smith, who simply wrote: "He was my friend."

Myrta Alice Little Davies was more successful as a professional writer than Lovecraft, at least in the short term. Before her marriage, she produced a constant stream of greeting card texts, poems, and short stories that ran nationally in newspapers and magazines. Her productivity tapered off after marriage because of her son's poor health, but even after his death in 1953, and the death of her husband three years later, she continued to publish children's stories for such markets as the *Christian Science Monitor*. In her late sixties, even in failing health, she continued to write op-ed pieces for the *Portsmouth Herald* about holidays. Only her death in 1967 silenced her pen.

Edgar Jacobs Davis passed the Massachusetts Bar in 1943 and soon opened an office in Merrimac Square. Not surprisingly, his office was above his father's hardware store. This location allowed Edgar to help in the family business as he attempted to gain his father's approval. Edgar died in his sleep of a heart attack at the family summer cottage on nearby Lake Attitash on 2 January 1949. He was forty-one and had suffered heart ailments for several years.

Left: Burial plot of Myrta Alice Little Davies. *Right:* The Davis family plot in Maplewood Cemetery. *Both photos courtesy Scott T. Goudsward.*

Before their friend and mentor was even cold in the ground, Wandrei and Derleth decided to publish a collection of Lovecraft's works.[2] *The Outsider and Others* was released in 1939 and was the first book published by Arkham House; 1,268 copies were printed.

Well aware that the published version of "The Shadow out of Time" had been modified by *Astounding Stories* and that no carbon copy of the typescript was made, Derleth and Wandrei obtained one of Lovecraft's personally corrected copies of the magazine to transcribe for the book. Although not credited as a co-editor, R. H. Barlow assisted with the creation of *Outsider,* theoretically in the role of literary executor. Tensions were growing as Arkham House attempted to bully its way into ownership of all Lovecraft's papers and copyrights. Wandrei in particular felt that Barlow had stolen Lovecraft's papers. But in accordance with Lovecraft's wishes, Barlow had taken some books for his personal collection, removed some papers, and donated others to Brown University, as the start of the recognized master repository of Lovecraft research material. Derleth did credit Barlow for contributions in other projects, but tensions continued to escalate. It came to a head; lawyers became involved and nothing was ever resolved.[3] Barlow was ostracized among Lovecraft's friends, and Derleth assumed control of Lovecraft's work as if Arkham House owned the literary rights by having the heirs of Lovecraft's aunt Annie Gamwell grant permission and then getting *Weird Tales* to transfer the copyrights it held.[4]

Neither Derleth nor Wandrei was aware that Lovecraft had given Barlow the notebook manuscript of "The Shadow out of Time" after he had typed the text, and he cannot be blamed for not mentioning it to them. Instead, Arkham House used Lovecraft's partially edited but still corrupt copy of the story. As late as Arkham House's 1984 collection, *The Dunwich Horror and Others*, "best guess" corrections were being made.

Arkham House had only an error-riddled transcription for the abridged appearance of Lovecraft's *The Case of Charles Dexter Ward* in *Weird Tales* (May–June 1941) and its subsequent appearance in Arkham House's 1943 *Beyond the Wall of Sleep*. Barlow "coincidentally" sent the manuscript to Brown University soon after the story was submitted to *Weird Tales*.

Barlow had been given the original "The Shadow out of Time" manuscript in 1935 and it was assumed to still be in his possession when he relocated to Mexico City College, where he eventually became chairman of the anthropology department. However, the notebook was not found among his papers when he died in 1951, leaving "The Shadow out of Time" the only major work of Lovecraft with no original manuscript or typescript.

As Arkham House began releasing more titles, W. Paul Cook wrote an article in 1945 warning that Lovecraft's legacy was being tarnished by "indiscriminate and even unintelligent praise, by lack of unbiased and intelligent criticism," warning that Derleth and Arkham House, by treating Lovecraft's lesser works as masterpieces, was delaying Lovecraft's recognition as a master of literature.[5] Derleth attempted to turn the cautionary article into a public feud, seeking to ostracize Cook as he had done to Robert Barlow. However, Barlow was a lesser known figure in Lovecraft's circle; W. Paul Cook was a beloved and respected icon of amateur journalism. Cook continued to be an ink-stained Cassandra and staunch advocate of Lovecraft until his own death in 1948.

Detail of Newburyport's MBTA station showing the brownstone arches salvaged from the YMCA building.

Brown University's John Hay Library received a fax on 17 January 1995, from a man in Kailua, Hawaii. He had been settling his late sister's estate and had found something that made the archivist catch his breath. Nelson Shreve, the gentleman in question, believed it was the long lost manuscript of "The Shadow out of Time."

The notebook arrived soon after. It was filled with 65½ pages of handwritten text, laboriously jotted down in pencil. The front page has a note "Begun Nov. 10, 1934," and on the final page is written, "Finished Feby. 22, 1935" and "Revised Feby. 24, 1935."

As best can be reconstructed, Barlow had indeed brought the notebook with him when he accepted a teaching position at Mexico City College. When it was not found among his effects after his death in 1951, it was presumed lost. Barlow apparently had lent the manuscript to June Ripley, one of his post-graduate students studying the Nahuatl language, Barlow's specialty. Ripley remained in Mexico until 1958 and then returned to the United States. After thirty-five years of teaching at schools across the country, she retired to Hawaii in 1993. She died on December 28, 1994, and the manuscript was discovered by her sister and brother-in-law while breaking up her estate.

S. T. Joshi immediately compared the handwritten notes to the published copies, discovering missing words and paragraphing discrepancies as expected. Unexpected was the discovery that there were also two full sentences of omitted text. A restored version of "The Shadow out of Time" appeared from Hippocampus Press in 2001, the first time the story of Haverhill's Nathaniel Wingate Peaslee was told exactly as Lovecraft had written it.

*   *   *

Today, Lovecraft would barely recognize Newburyport at first glance, but he might be pleased at the number of buildings that still survive. The downtown continued a steady decline into the late 1960s, when it appeared that the city would accept Federal Urban Renewal funds to raze the downtown and rebuild it from scratch. Preservationists convinced the city to cancel the plans. Instead, Newburyport accepted a federal grant that ensured the survival and renovation of the downtown area. Spared the urban renewal wrecking ball, Newbury-port's downtown has emerged as a trendy tourist destination of vibrant arts, charming shops, and fine dining. The ancient homes and buildings have been carefully restored, and it is difficult now to recognize the shabby-genteel town that had entranced Lovecraft and inspired Innsmouth.

Haverhill, however, would now be anathema to Lovecraft. The city accepted any and all available urban renewal funding in the 1960s and 1970s and proceeded to destroy nearly every structure with any age or character, particularly along Main Street. Nearly everything was leveled between Merrimack and Summer streets. The vibrant neighborhoods and the heart of the city became a giant dustbowl. The wounds to the city's psyche have still not healed. When urban renewal funds dried up, so did any potential for the downtown to become a destination for commerce or recreation.

Where Lovecraft once strolled down Washington Street from Railroad Square, the Queen Anne buildings, once home to shops and businesses, are protected historic treasures that house an endless line of restaurants, providing fine dining opportunities but with no other reason to go downtown.

Tryout Smith's box factory and the rest of Fleet Street became part of the expanded and underused GAR Park, a temporary measure that has become a permanent and futile tribute to anticipated new construction that never came. The Haverhill Public Library on Summer Street, also among the urban renewal casualties, was replaced with a new structure on Main Street. The local history collection, once considered one of the finest in the state, is only open a few hours per week, crippled by funding and staffing woes. This vaunted collection of local history contains a scant handful of issues of Smith's publication, the *Monthly Visitor,* and no issues of the *Tryout.* Smith's own immense collection of amateur journals now resides at the New York Public Library, where it forms the cornerstone of that institution's amateur journalism holdings. (Digitization of those journals began in 2013.)

There are still a few scattered landmarks remaining in the Merrimack Valley that were visited by, and inspirational to, H. P. Lovecraft. But the influence of Old Newbury and Pentucket exceeds architecture and landmarks. The *Tryout* was an incubator for Lovecraft's career. Although his contributions to the amateur journal of C. W. Smith were primarily poems of varying merit, they were published and shared among other writers, giving Lovecraft confidence to explore other forms and markets and to build a correspondence network that became a support group of writers that included such future luminaries as Fritz Leiber and Robert Bloch.

Lovecraft was buried in the Phillips plot, next to his parents, in Providence's Swan Point cemetery. In 1977, fans chipped in to pay for a headstone that, besides bearing his name and dates of birth and death, includes a simple declaration from his letters: "I Am Providence."[6] There is no question that Lovecraft himself believed it wholeheartedly. But it is also true that his works were amalgamations of impressions from his travels. Without Newburyport, there would be no Innsmouth, and without Haverhill's venerable Tryout

The Phillips family monument in Swan Point Cemetery in Providence.

Smith and his hapless typography, there arguably might not have been a Lovecraft. Providence may have been an integral part of Lovecraft's psyche, but the Merrimack Valley permeates his work.

APPENDIXES

Appendix A
THE HAVERHILL CONVENTION

By H. P. Lovecraft

Originally published in the *Tryout,* July 1921

Of the various shrines renowned in the annals of amateur journalism, none surpasses in importance that which bears the title of 408 Groveland St., Haverhill, Mass. It is here that *Tryout* is issued faithfully from month to month, and here that C. W. Smith, leader in publishing enterprise since 1889, presides like a patron deity over an Arcadian domain.

Yet notwithstanding these things, 408 Groveland St. still remains a *terra incognita* to most amateurs. Like the forbidden city of some royal dynasty, it is sacred ground, trodden only by the elect. Now and then some favoured mortal makes the pilgrimage and returns, but the number of such pilgrims is not great. It is therefore scarcely to be wondered at that a pardonable pride fills the souls of those who, on the afternoon of Thursday, June 9 [1921], participated in the unofficial Haverhill convention.

This convention was, in truth, not large; consisting only of the host, his learned and brilliant author-neighbour, Miss Myrta Alice Little, A. M., of Hampstead, N. H., Historian-Elect of the U.A.P.A, and the undersigned; together with Thomas Tryout, the Official Cat, and small Annette, the Official Mascot. In enthusiasm, however, it atoned for its slender attendance; for, as may be imagined, there is amateurical inspiration in every cubic inch of the atmosphere of the *Tryout* office. Each delegate is eager for a repetition of the event on a longer scale.

My own credentials for admission to this conclave were those of a servitor and scribbler. For some years I have been attached to the *Tryout* staff as rhymester, rhyme-collector, historian, and proofreader (of limited sections only), and had naturally acquired an increasing desire to behold with physical eye my benevolent "boss" and his publishing plant. Was not my one and only "book," "Looking Backward", here given the immortality of print? Now the hour had arrived, and guided by the new lettered luminary whose kind invitation had brought me north, and whose delightful family had royally entertained me at Little Towers in Hampstead, I entered the Elysian meads and groves of *Regio Tryoutiana*. Haverhill, let me add, is the most delectable of disappointments. Prepared to behold a dingy manufacturing town, the traveller is astonished by a city of beautiful homes, lawns, trees and gardens; in taste and attractiveness second to none. Amid such an environment, it is not strange that Tryout should possess its delightfully Doric air of pastoral grace.

Flanked by fertile flower and vegetable gardens, and blessed with a background of mystical faun-peopled woods dear to the editor's heart, stands the pleasant cottage numbered 408 Groveland St. In the rear, reached by a broad verdure-bordered path, is the Holy of Holies—*Tryout* office. Here, with walls made colourful by pictures, stamps, buttons, post-cards, and countless other accumulations of delightful nature, rests the faithful *Tryout* press with its type-cases, piles of paper, files, and other accessories, the whole establishment ruled by the genial editor.

To do justice here to Mr. Charles W. Smith is impossible, since it is he who will put these remarks into type; so I will content myself by describing *Tryout's* creator as a slender, wholesome, outdoor-looking man. He claims to have been born many centuries B.C., but in aspect and carriage nothing but youth is suggested. From his trim iron-grey hair and beard, and erect, well-proportioned form, one might pronounce him forty-five or fifty; yet he vows that this is a gross underestimation. Mr. Smith is a shining embodiment of those doctrines which teach the blessings of contentment and rural retirement. As Mr. Pope hath it:

"Happy the man whose wish and care
    A few paternal acres bound;
Content to breathe his native air,
    In his own ground.

* * * *

Sleep by night; study and ease,
    Together mix'd; sweet recreation;
And innocence, which most does please
    With meditation."[1]

Gifted with health, our Tryout is never idle or listless; but spends his days as Nature intended, at once pleasing himself and conferring pleasure on others. He is a monarch in his fair domain; a spirit ever youthful, constantly revivified by his quiet pursuits—editing, printing, walking, exploring "Whittierland", stamp-collecting, and conversing with his grandchild-mascot and playful nine-year-old Thomas cat. He recalls the familiar lines of the Mantuan swain:

"Tityre, tu patulae recubans sub tegmine fagi
Silvestrem tennui Musam meditaris avena;
Nos patriae finis et dulcia linquimus arva;
Nos patriam fugimus: tu, Tityre, lentus in umbra,
Formosam resonare doces Amaryllida silvas."[2]

Mr. Smith's own writing reflects much of this Arcadian colour in inimitable fashion, and it is to be regretted that he does not allot a large portion of magazine space for such quaint and unforgettable essays as "Anent the Melancholy Days" and "Scared? No-o-o!"

Two hours is all too brief an interval for a full-sized convention, but much can be compressed therein amidst an atmosphere as saturated with amateur tradition as it that of *Tryout* office. Files of *Tryouts* and *Monthly Visitors* were produced, old convention photographs studied, and vain inquiries made as to the identity of "Lester Kirk" and "Dame Gossip." The meeting of two Merrimack Valley leaders like Miss Little and Mr. Smith, representing the newest as well as the oldest traditions of the amateur world, should augur well for future local activity, especially since another gifted Haverhill litterateur is about to join the ranks of the United.

Altogether, the Haverhill convention was a decided success. Washington and Boston may furnish imitations impressive in point of numbers, yet neither can command so central a position in the ocean of amateur efforts. *Tryout* is the social lifeblood and nervous system of the fraternity today; if any doubt it, let him try to picture an amateurdom devoid of this indispensable bond and inspiration.

Appendix B
FIRST IMPRESSIONS OF NEWBURYPORT

By H. P. Lovecraft

Extract from a letter to Samuel Loveman dated 29 April 1923[1]

Embarked for Newburyport, the car took us through some of the choicest scenery of New England, for in this northerly region the hills are gently & graceful, & unexpected vistas of village roofs & spires are frequent. Commerce & manufacturers have not destroyed the quiet simplicity of the inhabitants, & they still dream the years away amidst scenes but little altered by the passing centuries. Crossing Chain Bridge—the oldest suspension bridge in America—we approached the suburbs of Newburyport & began to get whiffs & glimpses of the neighbouring sea, & to descry the ancient houses & chimney-pots of the famous town which, though said a century and a quarter ago to possess a social life more cultivated & brilliant than that of Washington, is today locally known as the "City of the Living Dead".

Up the narrow street we rattled—deciding to stick to the one-man car for a preliminary panorama, & to defer the pedestrian exploring until later. Ineffably quaint & archaic are the Georgian streets which we saw from the windows—fascinating hills lined with venerable dwellings of every description, from 200-year-old hovels huddled together in nondescript groups with rambling extensions & lean-to's, to stately Colonial mansions with proud gables & magnificent doorways. One feature possessed in common by nearly all the houses, great & humble alike, was the curious old-world abundance of chimney-pots, here more prevalent even than in magic Marblehead! All at once the car reached a spacious square, lined on every side with the quaint brick mercantile buildings of the Revolutionary period. It was a sight such as we had never seen before—a city business section of the 18th century, preserved in every detail. As the car passed on, entering again a delicious maze of ancient streets & turning almost every corner in sight, we wondered when we should reach the modern business section; but after a time the houses thinned out & we found ourselves speeding past the shanties . . . of fisherman toward the salt marshes of the open country to the south, with the sand-choked harbour on our left, & the long stretch of Plum Island in the distance beyond. Then we questioned the driver, & discovered the truth of a suspicion which had crossed our minds but fleetingly before. It was really so—that Georgian business section was in truth the business section of today as well! You saw it, I think, on the joint card Davis & I sent you—can you imagine the reality? The commercial Newburyport of 1780 still stands. . . . truly, a City of the Living Dead!

Upon alighting from the car, at the end of the route, we strolled back through the maze of picturesque streets; ecstatically drinking in the antique houses of wood, brick, & stone, with peaked, gambrel, or flat roofs, massive or graceful chimneys, quaint chimney-pots, & artistic Colonial doorways. It was the past brought to life—flashes of 18th century bye-streets, silhouettes of Christopher Wren steeples, kaleidoscopic etchings of old-time skylines, snatches of glistening harbour beyond delectably rambling & alluringly antediluvian alleys that wind lazily down hill—a true paradise of the born antiquarian! Once we walked the whole length of a ramshackle alley without losing for a second the illusion of the Colonial age of sea-power. Through a cross-alley we saw the splendid facade & columns of a stone mansion in the distance—engaging vista! Thoughts of the past welled up—here were the lodgings of adventurous sailors who knew the far Indies & the perfumed East, & there dwelt a solid, periwigged captain whose skill had led many a sturdy barque around the Horn, or through Magellan's tortuous strait, or past the Cape of Good Hope. Then we went down to the rotting wharves & dreamed of old days, & in fancy saw the heaps of cordage & bales of strange Asian wares, & the forest of masts that reached half across to Plum Island. Ah, me—the days that were! After this we returned to the business section, bought some cards, & set out for famous & opulent High St., where stands the old mansion of the celebrated eccentric Timothy Dexter.

You must have heard of Dexter & his lucky speculations, attempts to enter society, freakish extravagance, grotesque house & grounds, ridiculous escapades, hilarious pretensions to titled aristocracy, liveried poet-laureate, (an ex-fishmonger, the D. V. Bush of his day)[2] outdoor museum of wooden statues, (including one of himself, labelled "I am first in the East, first in the West, & the greatest philosopher of the Western World") & absurd book called "A Pickle for the Knowing Ones". That book was misspelled & unpunctuated; & when people objected to the latter feature, "Lord" Dexter published a second edition, (1796) still unpunctuated, but with a page of assorted punctuation marks at the end, plus the note:

> "mister printer the Nowing Ones complane of my book the fust edition had no stops I put in A Nuf here & thay may peper & solt it as thay plese."

In our family there is an old print of Dexter's house, made in 1810, four years after his death, & shewing the ludicrous ornaments & the statues of celebrities atop the fence-posts. Today, however, all the extravagances are decorously removed; & all that one sees of Dexter's follies are the oddly turned columns by the doorway, & the gilt eagle atop the cupola.

Strolling south from Dexter's mansion, Edgar & I noted the ancient churchyard & the new church going up within it. That edifice will mark Newburyport's awakening to the great aesthetic truth which Salem has always realized namely, that every old town has its architectural atmosphere, to which all new buildings must conform. In the hideous Victorian age of tastelessness, nearly every town but Salem was ruined by the construction of ugly nondescript buildings like New York's post-office, &c. Salem alone knew the need for harmonious congruity, & stuck to classical & Colonial models. But just now Newburyport is waking up, & is trying to reclaim its heritage. In this old churchyard, where once a Colonial belfry saluted the sky, an ugly neo-Gothic church was built some time in the 19ᵗʰ century when the original structure decayed or burned. It was horribly out of place in Newburyport—but what could you expect of Victorian times? Now—Pegāna[3] be prais'd—taste has reappeared; & the Gothick monstrosity hath been torn down to make way for a beautiful new stone edifice on the simple & classical lines of the original Georgian structure. Gloria in excelsis! Once more the ancient slabs will look up to noble walls in harmony with their atmosphere, & the quiet corner—where a venerable bye-street slopes shadily & beckoningly down from the travell'd way—will assume again that immemorial tranquillity which comes only to such old regions as grow in organic fashion, building cell by cell from the vital impulses of elder aeons.

Still further south we went, admiring the stately mansions of old captains of the sea, with the tall cupolas where they used to scan the distant waves with spyglasses. Good old days! Providence has some of those cupola'd houses—on the old hill overlooking the bay, which you must see some time. Salem has many, but Newburyport probably has most of all. On a side street we found an old house whose lower floor was being converted into a shop. The new shop window, with its glassless frame & broad seat, invited us; & we sate down for a long rest, gazing at ancient houses—one fully 250 years old—& stately, gigantic elm trees.

But time was flying, & it was getting damn cold. We had now reached a point which involved a retracing of those quaint, narrow streets & alleys we had first explored; & delightedly we went about it, pausing now & then to admire some particularly picturesque scenic effect—whether of quaintness, magnificence, or antique decay. Reaching once more the central square, we partook of a meal at the one decent restaurant in the "city", (the cafe of the more-than-a-century-old Adams House) where for 65¢ apiece we were served with more than I could eat. (Clark's Lunches & Mills' & Chapin's Cafeterias please take notice!) Finally filled, we took the car back to Merrimac; where after an evening of discussion we dispersed—to meet but briefly the next morning before Edgar hustled off to high school.

Appendix C
TRYOUT'S RETURN TO HAVERHILL

Plaistow, N.H.

by C. W. Smith

Originally published in the *Tryout,* December 1926

Some four years ago I was "sentenced" to spend two years in Plaistow, N. H. Usually one "doing time" gets time off for good behavior, but as I served four, instead of two years, I must have been an unruly prisoner.

In a way I rather enjoyed my sojourn in this pretty little village, but my "Heart was hitched to Haverhill," and

"Old places have a charm for me
    The new can ne'er attain.
Old faces how I long to see,
    Their kindly looks again."[1]

Plaistow appealed to me in some ways, I liked its open spaced, and its bits of wood-land scattered in and about the village, and I even enjoyed my walks over its dirt, and often dusty, muddy, brush bordered roads.

Plaistow is situated in the south eastern part of the Granite State, on the line dividing Mass. from New Hampshire. I learn from the Gazetteer of New Hampshire, issued in 1817, that it was settled in 1764. At the date the Gazetteer was published it had 462 inhabitants, and that it contains 6839 acres. It was formerly part of Haverhill, Mass. being included in the Indian purchase of 1642.

Its principle [*sic*] street, Main Street, extends north and south through the village for quite a distance. It is bordered with large elms, and presents an attractive appearance.

But little business is carried on in the village. Its inhabitants are generally devoted to agriculture, although some of them find employment in the Haverhill shoe factories, making the trip—about 4 miles—by electrics.

One remarkable thing about Plaistow is that of the many large lakes and ponds within the Granite State, there are none in Plaistow. There are only two mill ponds of about an acre each.

I am glad to be at home again and amid familiar haunts. I have had

> "Enough of briary wood, and hot chalk-down."

And longed

> "To hear the gay glad hum of town."[2]

The Return

by H. P. Lovecraft

Originally published in the *Tryout,* December 1926

The sun with brighter beams on high
    Lights up the Merrimack's swift rill.
And village bells in chorus cry,
    "TRYOUT is back in Haverhill!"

The friendly roofs and steeples ring
    With echoes of the cordial strain,
For one who from long voyaging
    Today is welcom'd home again,

Familiar hills his feet invite,
    And conscious streets his presence tell,

Pleas'd with the fond, remember'd sight
    Of him who loves their winding well.

In neighb'ring forests, glades, and meads,
    The sprightly fauns their brother hail,
And Pan awaits 'mid lakeside reeds
    His long-miss'd step, with rod and pail.

The orchards bend with grateful fruits,
    And autumn boughs resplendent blaze;
While the late autumn gorgeous shoots
    Thro' sunset-fir'd October haze.

Hail to our TRYOUT'S nimble tread!
    Hail to his song of clanking steel,
As the neat page so fondly read
    Anew his busy hours reveal!

May joy inspire the hearthside flame
    That lights its master's form once more
And peace a full dominion claim
    Round the snug walls and cottage door.

Back to his own! There let him bask
    Long in the scenes he holds so dear;
Blest with whate'er his soul may ask
    To fill each happy, home-like year!

Appendix D

THE PUBLISHED WORKS OF MYRTA ALICE LITTLE DAVIES

Compiled by David Goudsward and Chris Perridas

Lovecraft's long popularity notwithstanding, Myrta Alice Little Davies was the more successful professional writer. Her published work exceeds Lovecraft's in quantity and profitability. The following list does not include her contributions to the amateur press, but it does include op-ed columns to illustrate the length of her career. Dates of syndicated material are based on copyright notice, not date of first appearance. Several of the syndicated pieces appeared in various papers nationally over a two- to three-year period.

Prior to 1903 per Hampstead Town History, *source unknown*
"Miss Violet's Thirteen"
"Him that cometh unto Me I will in no wise cast out"
"Theresa"

1920—Syndicated (McClure Newspaper Syndicate)
"The Fourth" (as Myrta Alice Little)
"The Leader" (MAL)
"Marvel Day" (MAL)
"First Stop, Lady" (MAL)
"Palms or Apple" (MAL)
"Matchmaker" (MAL)

1920—*The Kindergarten-Primary Magazine* (February 1920)
"Away to Babyland!" (poem) (MAL)

1920—*The Kindergarten-Primary Magazine* (May 1920)
"Daddy Brought Them" (poem) (MAL)
"A Pet" (poem) (MAL)
"Altogether Lovely" (poem) (MAL)
"In the Fall" (poem) (MAL)

1921—"Air" (MAL)
Syndicated (McClure Newspaper Syndicate)

1921—*The Kindergarten-Primary Magazine* (November–December 1921)
"The Thanksgiving Surprise" (as M. A. Little)

1922—All syndicated (McClure Newspaper Syndicate)
"On The Train" (MAL)
"Mosquitoes" (MAL)
"Ralpha and the 'Stop' Sign" (MAL)

1922— *The Kindergarten-Primary Magazine* (September 1922)
"The Most Beautiful Princess" (poem) (MAL)

1923—All syndicated (McClure Newspaper Syndicate)
"Out" (MAL)
"Marvel Day" (MAL)
"Little Things" (MAL)
"Susan's Evidence" (MAL)
"Ben Was Awakened at Last" (as Myrta Davies)

1924—All syndicated (McClure Newspaper Syndicate)
"An Engagement Well Received" (MD)
"'Violet Acres'—Their Tea-Room" (MD)

1927—Syndicated (McClure Newspaper Syndicate)
"Ginger" (as Myrta Little Davies)

1927—Syndicated (McClure Newspaper Syndicate)
"By Their Deeds" (as Myrta Alice Little Davies)

1928—Syndicated (McClure Newspaper Syndicate)
"The Mystery of Hermit Hut" (MLD)

1928—*Christian Science Monitor*
"The Story about the Play-House" (MLD) June 25
"The Story about the Haying Party" (MLD) July 30
"The Story about Going to the Beach" (MLD) August 20

1929— *Christian Science Monitor* (December 12)
"Rebekah Anne Decides" (MLD)

1929—*Sweet Christmas Time* (2-scene pageant) by MLD
Eldridge Entertainment House, Franklin, OH

1934—*New England Short Stories* 2 (1934)
"A Queen Did It" (MLD)

1941—*New Hampshire Troubadour* (April)
"Hobnobbing With Hobbies" (MLD)

1943—*Hobbies* (September)
"Taking the Bite out of Buttons" (MLD)

1949—Hampstead 200th Anniversary souvenir booklet
"Ode to an Old District School" (poem) (MLD)

1954—*Portsmouth* [NH] *Herald* (April 7)
"Remembrance" (op-ed column) (MLD)

1954—*Springfield* [MA] *Sunday Republican* (April 11)
"Easter Eve and Easter Dawn" (op-ed page poem) (MLD)
"Easter Rainbow" (poem)

1955—*Portsmouth Herald* (February 11)
"St. Valentine's" (op-ed column) (MLD)

1955—*Portsmouth Herald* (March 23)
"Another Easter" (op-ed column) (MLD)

1955—*Springfield Sunday Republican* (April 10)
"Easter Magic" (op-ed page poem) (MLD)

1961—*Bar Harbor* [MA] *Times* (January 26)
"How Do I Know That My Youth Is Not Spent" (poem)
(Myrta Little Davies, Colby, '08)

Appendix E
HOWARD PRESCOTT LOVECRAFT

C. W. Smith in the *Tryout*, April 1937.
(with minor tryoutisms corrected)

"Death Loves a Shining Mark." I don't know who is the author of that proverb,[1] but it never was more strongly emphasized than the praising of Howard Prescott Lovecraft.

A genius has been taken from among us. If there were ever one in amateur journalism, it was Howard Prescott Lovecraft.

Over twenty years correspondence with him, and numerous personal meetings, revealed to me his many characteristics—his integrity, his gentlemanly deportment and his keen literary attainments. We had many things in common. Love of the open, old books, historical houses and papers, and even the lowly (?) cat was a bond between us. Many of his first contributions to the amateur press appeared in Tryout and he continued to contribute to it until his professional work required most of his time. Still I never requested a favor of him but he willingly granted it. His "Looking Backward" first printed in Tryout and reproduced in pamphlet form—him who is fortunate enough to possess a copy has a classic in amateur publications. I regret his passing and feel that in his death I have met with a personal loss, as well others who have come in contact with him either personally or through correspondence. I have written of him as he impressed me. Of his literary work I leave to more competent pen than mine to estimate. That it was of the highest none will gainsay.

Of him a correspondent writes:

News of the death of Howard Lovecraft will be received with the deepest regret by Amateurdom the world over. To many of the large circle of correspondents who had come to appreciate the sterling worth of the man, his genuineness of mind and heart, the unfailing uprightness of his views and acts, his large capacity for friendship, to many of these the news of his death will bring a sense of personal sorrow and loss. I am terribly shaken and shocked. I have lost one of my closest and dearest friends in Amateurdom.

Appendix F
THE PUBLICATIONS OF CHARLES W. SMITH

Because of the ephemeral nature of amateur journalism, this list should not be considered complete. Items marked with question marks are unconfirmed as to date or existence, but they are included based on apparent numbering. All publications are from Haverhill, MA, unless noted otherwise. Items of note by Smith and Lovecraft are indicated as appropriate. A comprehensive list of Lovecraft items was not attempted because of quantity and multiple pseudonyms.

This list is based partially on a checklist of papers compiled by the Library of Amateur Journalism compiled for the January 1943 edition of *Boys' Herald.*

The Boys' Companion
V. 1, No. 1–4, 1872

The Jolly Joker
V. 1, No. 1–2, 1872

The Nonpareil
V. 1, No. 1–4, 1871
V. 2, No. 1–4, 1872
V. 3, No. 1–4, 1873

The Tyro
Co-edited with C. S. Ellis; published in Worcester, MA
V. 1   No. 1, February 20, 1878
       No. 2

No. 3, April 20, 1878
No. 4, May 20, 1878
June
July
August
September
October
November/December

Pick Me Up
Dates and volumes unknown. Its existence is confirmed by Smith in his autobiographical notes in the January 1943 edition of *Boys' Herald.*

The Monthly Visitor
Published as F. H. Smith & Co
  V. 1, No. 1–12, January–December 1888
  V. 2, No. 1–12, January–December 1889
  V. 3, No. 1–12, January–December 1890
  V. 4, No. 1–12, January–December 1891
  V. 5, No. 1–12, January–December 1892
  V. 6, No. 1–12, January–December 1893
Published as Charles W. Smith
  V. 7, No. 1–12, January–December 1894
  V. 8, No. 1–12, January–December 1895
  V. 9, No. 1–12, January–December 1896
  V. 10, No. 1–6, January–July 1897
  No. 7, August 1897 (misdated as 1899)

The Nightingale
Supplement to the *Monthly Visitor* V. 5, no 7 (July 1892)

The Bay State Official
Massachusetts Amateur Press Association quarterly
Supplement to the *Monthly Visitor* V. 4, no. 3 (March 1891), V. 4, no. 6 (June 1891), V. 7, no. 3 (March 1894), V. 8, no. 4 (April 1895)

The Tryout

V. 1   No. 1, December 1914. No volume or issue listed; "issued occasionally by C. W. Smith."

No. 2–12, January–November 1915

V. 2   No. 1, December 1915

No. 2–4, January–March 1916

No. 5, April 1916, "The Power of Wine: A Satire." HPL's first poem in the *Tryout*.

No. 6–12, May–November 1916

THE TRYOUT

VOL 18   HAAERHILL, MASS.   NQ. 6.

THE SEASON OF BY AND BY.

○

I KNOW a picture with pigments
Purer than those of the sky,
When the crimson of dawn
Are bright there thereon.
I will paint it—By and By.
I know of a song that is sweeter
Than any song that fly
Through the blue air in a thrushes heart,
1 will sing it—By and By.
I know of a stature grander
In the wondrous realms of art, precious.
I will carve it—By and By.
The wheels of Time run onward,
The seasons fade and fly,
But the dimmest star in the house of Time
Will never be By and By.

Visitor.   **Arthur Goodenough.**

C. W. SMITH.   HAVERHILL, MASS.

V. 3   No. 1, December 1916
        No. 2, January 1917
        No. 3–12, February–November 1917
        No. 1, December 1917
        No. 2–12, January–November 1918

V. 5   No. 1, January 1919 (misidentified as V. 4)
        No. 2–12, February–December 1919

V. 6   No. 1, January 1920, "Tryout's Lament for the Vanished Spider"
        (HPL)
        No. 2, February 1920, "Looking Backward" 1 (HPL)
        No. 3, March 1920, "Looking Backward" 2 (HPL)
        No. 4, April 1920, "Looking Backward" 3 (HPL)
        No. 5, May 1920, "Looking Backward" 4 (HPL)
        No. 6, June 1920, "Looking Backward" 5 (HPL), "At Rest:
        Susan Boynton Britton." (CWS)
        No. 7, July 1920 (printed with no date)
        No. 8, August 1920 (misidentified No. 7)
        No. 9–10, September–October 1920
        No. 11, November 1920, "The Cats of Ulthar" (HPL)
        No. 12, December 1920

V. 7   No. 1–5, February–June 1921
        No. 6, July 1921, "The Terrible Old Man" (HPL), "The Haver-
        hill Convention" (HPL)
        No. 7, October 1921, "The Tree" (HPL)
        No. 8, November 1921
        No. 9, December 1921, "Sir Thomas Tryout" (HPL)
        No. 10–11, February–March 1922
        No. 12, May 1922

V. 8   No. 1–3, July–September 1922
        No. 4–7, January–April 1923 (published in Plaistow, NH)
        No. 8, June 1923
        No. 9–12, August–December 1923

V. 9   No. 1–5, January–May 1924
        No. 6–10, July–December 1924
        No. 11, January 1925
        No. 12, March 1925

V. 10   No. 1–2, April–May 1925
        No. 3–5, July–September 1925
        No. 6, November 1925 "In the Vault" (HPL)
        No. 7, January 1926
        No. 8–12, March–July 1926

V. 11   No. 1, December 1926, published in Haverhill, MA: "The Re-
        turn" (HPL), "Plaistow, N.H." (CWS)
        No. 2, January 1927
        No. 3–5, March–May 1927
        No. 6–7, July–August 1927
        No. 8, September 1927, "The Trip of Theobald" (HPL)
        No. 9, November 1927
        No. 10, December 1927 (misidentified as No. 11)
        No. 11, January 1928
        No. 12, March 1928

V. 12   No. 1, April 1928
        No. 2–6, June–October 1928
        No. 7, December 1928
        No. 8, January 1929
        No. 9, March 1929
        No. 10–12, May–July 1929

V. 13   No. 1–5, August–December 1929
        No. 6, January 1930
        No. 7–11, June–October 1930
        No. 12, December 1930

V. 14   No. 1–7, May–November 1931
        No. 8, February 1932
        No. 9–12, April–July 1932

V. 15   No. 1–5, August–December 1932
No. 6, January 1933
No. 7, March 1933
No. 8–12, May–September 1933

V. 16   No. 1, October 1933
No. 2, December 1933
No. 3, March 1934 (misidentified as No. 5)
No. 4–5, April–May 1934
No. 6–7, July–August 1934
No. 8, September 1934 "In Memory: Edith May Miniter. A Coworker in Amateur Journalism. 1884–1934." Issued by Laurie A. Sawyer and C. W. Smith
No. 9, October 1934
No. 10, December 1934
No. 11, January? 1935 (published with no month)
No. 12, March 1935

V. 17   No. 1, May? 1935 (published with no month)
No. 2–6, June–October 1935
No. 7, December 1935
No. 8, January 1936
No. 9, March 1936
No. 10–12, May.–July 1936

V. 18   No. 1–3, September–December 1936
No. 4, January 1937
No. 5, March 1937
No. 6, April? 1937 (published with no month), "Howard Prescott Lovecraft" (CWS)
No. 7–9, June–August 1937
No. 10–12, October–December 1937

V. 19   No. 1–2, February–March 1938
No. 3–4, May–June 1938

No. 5–6, August–September 1938
No. 7, November 1938
No. 8. January 1939 (misidentified as No. 7)
No. 9, March 1939 (misidentified as No. 8)
No. 10, April 1939 (misidentified as No. 9)
No. 11, May 1939 (misdated as June)
No. 12. June 1939

V. 20   No. 1, May 1939
No. 2–3, October–November 1939
No. 5–8, February–May 1940
No. 9, July 1940
No. 10, August 1940
No. 11, September? 1940
No. 12, December 1940

V. 21   No. 1–2, March–April 1941
No. 3, June 1941 (misidentified as V. 20)
No. 4, August 1941
No. 5, October 1941
No. 6, December 1941
No. 7, January 1942
No. 8, March 1942
No. 9–10, July–August 1942
No. 11, September 1942
No. 12, December 1942

V. 22   No.1, (date unkown)
No. 2, December 1943 (no volume or issue listed)
No. 3, Aug 1944 (no volume or issue listed) "From the Bed Room Printery"

Emerson Duerr attempted to continue the *Tryout*, publishing V. 22, No. 4 in August 1947 and four issues of a renumbered "New Series" between 1947 and 1949. He also published issues of *Tryout Junior* during the same period. Between the three titles, Duerr published no more than 7 or 8 issues of *Tryout,* compared to Smith's 255 issues.

V. 22, No. 4, August 1947, "Tryout Says" (CWS) (a notice about transition from Smith to Duerr as editor/publisher).

V. 1 No. 1 (NS), October 1947, "Ninety-Fifth Birthday Poem (CWS)

Pamphlets
The Lord of Monteith, or the, Secret of the Red Chamber
Richard Gerner.
Haverhill, MA: H. C. Smith & Co., Publishers & Prints, 1873.

The Curse of Passion, or, $10,000 Reward, Dead or Alive!
Richard Gerner.
Haverhill, MA: Charles W. Smith, 1873.

In Memory of Susan Brown Robbins, A Coworker in Amateur Journalism. 1891–1898. Issued by Edith Miniter and C. W. Smith
Haverhill, MA, [1911]

Looking Backward.
H. P. Lovecraft.
Haverhill, MA: C. W. Smith, 1920.

Poetical Melange: Anthology
C. W. Smith, ed.
[Haverhill, MA: C. W. Smith, 1928.]

Thoughts and Pictures.
Eugene B. Kuntz.
Co-operatively published by H. P. Loveracft [*sic*] and C. W. Smith.
Haverhill, MA: C. W. Smith, 1932.

Undated Apocrypha
Summer
Inward Music

Appendix G
H. P. LOVECRAFT, "THE DUNWICH HORROR," AND MYSTERY HILL

Mystery Hill is a megalithic site with archaeo-astronomical components. Located in North Salem, New Hampshire, it is open to the public as an open-air museum under the name America's Stonehenge. The possibility that horror and fantasy writer H. P. Lovecraft visited Mystery Hill has been a point of discussion for many years.

Researcher Andrew E. Rothovius was the first to make the suggestion that Mystery Hill or another of the New England grooved stone slabs was the inspiration for the sacrificial table on Sentinel Hill in "The Dunwich Horror." Rothovius mentions it as a passing thought in May 1964 in an article for *Yankee* on the various unidentified stone structures in New England.[1] This reference caught the attention of August Derleth, who asked him to elaborate in an article for *The Dark Brotherhood and Other Pieces,* a planned collection of Lovecraft's work supplemented by memoirs and criticism. In the interim, Rothovius researched the question from the Lovecraft side of the equation and decided that the stone slab in Hadley, within twenty-five miles of Wilbraham, was the most likely candidate. When *The Dark Brotherhood* came out in 1966, it contained Rothovius's "Lovecraft and the New England Megaliths" with the Hadley slab as the most likely inspiration of the altar stone atop Sentinel Hill in "The Dunwich Horror."[2]

The slab, resting outside the Hadley Farm Museum, is the largest of the known "sacrificial table" stones, measuring eight feet long and six and a half feet wide. One additional unusual feature is not found on the other sacrificial tables scattered across the region: this stone is the only stone with drainage runnels on two sides. This is a design feature not found on cider presses, tar burners, or lye stones and raises doubts on identifications that claim these slabs as such. The provenance of the stone is somewhat murky. Rothovius notes a local tradition that has it originating in neighboring Pelham at the start of the twentieth century in an area now submerged under the Quabbin Reservoir. Further complicating the matter, when Philip Shreffler visited Hadley in 1977, he was told it had been found "up near Goshen," twenty-five miles west of Pelham.[3] These two stories sound suspiciously like retellings regarding other artifacts found in the region, further adding questions about the Hadley stone's origin.[4]

Aerial shot of the "sacrificial table" at Mystery Hill as it would have appeared prior to 1937. Photo by Malcolm Pearson from *The Ruins of Great Ireland in New England* (1946) by William B. Goodwin.

The one certainty is that Lovecraft could not have visited the stone at Hadley Farm Museum in his 1928 pre-Dunwich visit to Wilbraham and Athol. The barn that houses the Hadley museum collection was not moved to its current location until 1930, and the museum did not open to the public until 1931. The stone itself did not arrive at the museum until 1957–61 during the time the museum was owned by the

Massachusetts Society for the Promotion of Agriculture, and their records do not indicate where it was acquired.

The only stone slab that could have been visited by Lovecraft becomes Rothovius's original thought—Mystery Hill. This shifts the primary focus of the discussion from where to when. Placement of the date of a potential visit determines whether Lovecraft might have used the North Salem megalithic ruins as part of the inspiration for the fictional ruins atop Sentinel Hill in "The Dunwich Horror."

H. Warner Munn, friend of Lovecraft and fellow fantasy writer, verified the fact of a visit by Lovecraft and himself, but the date, not remembered after more than fifty years years, must be placed by circumstantial evidence. W. H. Pugmire and Donald R. Burleson were individually in contact with Munn up to the time of Munn's death in 1981. Pugmire recalls Munn confirming a brief statement by L. Sprague de Camp noting that Munn had accompanied Lovecraft to Mystery Hill.[5]

Burleson's correspondence is more detailed and adds significant complications. Summarizing the correspondence between Munn and Burleson, Munn, his wife Malvina, and Lovecraft arrived in North Salem and were told where to find the caretaker. At the house, a "rather pretty" woman said she would bring them to the site. Upon arrival at an enclosure, she discovered that she had forgotten the key and made the suggestion that she and Munn return for it while Lovecraft and Mrs. Munn wait. Mrs. Munn was angry at the idea and said they would all go back or all go home. Munn estimates the visit took place prior to William Goodwin's purchase of the site, although he recalls evidence of digging and hearing the "Culdee Monk" theory. In a later letter, Munn reiterates both the enclosure and the female caretaker.[6]

January 1937 correspondence between site owner William B. Goodwin and his staff shows that the fence that still surrounds the site was being considered even before the land purchase was finalized.[7] Considering the difficulties involved in digging post holes and pouring cement in a New England winter, the fence probably was not started until after the sale of the land to Goodwin was finalized in April 1937, a month after Lovecraft's death.

Additionally, Goodwin bought the site after his first visit in July 1936, at which time he believed the stone ruins were a village site of a lost Norwegian colony from Western Greenland, circa 1344. Locally, the site's construction was attributed to the Pattee family who built a house over a section of stone structures. Goodwin changed his opinion soon after the purchase, deciding the site was the ruins of a Culdee monastery that was the hub of a regional attempt to convert the natives. The fence and Culdee monks definitely point to a date after Lovecraft's premature demise.

The date is further verified by the reference to the female caretaker. Burleson suggests that the mystery woman may have been neighborhood teen, Elsie Conley, who was interviewed about the caves by a reporter with the *Haverhill Evening Gazette* in 1934, but the 1937 or later date suggests another neighbor, Anna Abbotson.[8]

William B. Goodwin, a retired insurance executive and a noted collector of rare maps and colonial furniture, finalized his purchase of the site in 1937. Goodwin was a resident of Hartford, Connecticut, and seventy-one years old when he purchased the site. Being so far away meant visits were infrequent. So he hired Harry Abbotson as part of the crew employed to clean up the site. Since Abbotson lived around the corner from the site, on Spicket River Road, he also served as the winter caretaker and impromptu host if someone wished to see the ruins. Based on various letters from the time period, Abbotson's sister, Anna, who also lived in the family house, acted as hostess for Abbotson on numerous occasions. Although not employed by Goodwin, Anna was intimately involved with the site and, as such, more than capable of both leading groups to the site and discussing Goodwin's theories.[9] If Abbotson was not available, Anna would be the only other local resident with access to the key to unlock the gates and lead visitors to the site.

Munn obviously remembered touring the site, offering details not generally available in printed descriptions. But it would appear that after fifty years, he blurred details from two visits and is describing a visit to Mystery Hill that took place after Goodwin erected the fence, and which therefore had to occur after Lovecraft's death. Munn is also credited with a decidedly different account of the visit by Philip Shreffler in *The H. P. Lovecraft Companion:*

> It is with Munn that Lovecraft traveled to the archaeological site at Mystery Hill, New Hampshire, where, according to Munn himself, Lovecraft wandered among the stone ruins discoursing about his pantheon of timeless gods and how the monolithic setting would have suited them.[10]

This is in conflict with Munn's correspondence to Burleson in which he believes that Lovecraft was not overly impressed with the site.[11] Shreffler's reference is based on an oral interview with Munn in 1975. The discrepancy between the two recollections is further complicated by Munn himself, who had previously written a recollection of Lovecraft for Stuart David Schiff's magazine *Whispers*.[12] In this article, Munn describes a visit to Dogtown that, like the trip to Mystery Hill, is remembered by Munn but not recorded in the correspondence. Dogtown, between Gloucester and Rockport, is the forested ruins of an abandoned colonial settlement with only glacier boulders and abandoned cellar holes to mark its location.[13]

In the same article, Munn recalls the visit to "Pattee's Caves," the earlier name of Mystery Hill, and again describes the site in terms that could not exist until after Lovecraft's death. Munn describes sitting on the "sacrificial table," a difficult task given that the stone was flat on the ground until Goodwin's team removed the fill around it to expose the legs in the early 1940s. This, and the almost interchangeable references to both Dogtown and Mystery Hill, strengthens the supposition that Munn is blurring visits to Mystery Hill with details from Dogtown. The recollection in *Whispers* was written first (1976), the Shreffler interview was prior to his 1977 book, and the letters to Burleson date to 1979. The first piece is the only one to mention Dogtown, suggesting that Munn was combining multiple trips into one with each retelling, not entirely a surprise thirty or forty years after the fact. Further complicating the matter, Munn's correspondence with Lovecraft was destroyed.[14]

A current view of the "sacrificial table" at Mystery Hill.

Munn was first introduced to Lovecraft on 23 July 1927, when he accompanied W. Paul Cook on a visit with Lovecraft in Providence. Cook had met his fellow Athol resident in 1924 and discovered a connection to Lovecraft; Munn's first short story had been accepted by *Weird Tales.* "The Werewolf of Ponkert" (*Weird Tales,* July 1925) was inspired by a letter by Lovecraft in an earlier issue of *Weird Tales* pondering why no one had ever written a story from the werewolf's perspective. Lovecraft and Munn hit it off immediately, and Lovecraft suddenly had another correspondent.

The next summer, on a visit to Athol, Munn drove Lovecraft to see the Bear's Den, a lushly forested waterfall and cave in New Salem, about 20 miles southwest of Athol. Later that year, Lovecraft included "Cold Spring Glen" as a landmark in "The Dunwich Horror" based on Bear's Den.[15] Munn and Cook again visited Lovecraft in Providence and Lovecraft visited Athol with some regularity.

Cook's wife had died in January. He had suffered a breakdown and dropped contact with everyone. So when Lovecraft visited Athol in

June 1930, he stayed with the newly married Munn. In a letter to Donald Wandrei, Lovecraft notes: "I am staying with Munn—who is about to move to larger quarters on the edge of the village. Weather has been doubtful, but Munn has taken me to a number of scenic spots in his car."[16]

This is the most likely period for a visit to Mystery Hill (and Dogtown). It does raise another question: How did Munn and Lovecraft know of the Mystery Hill site? Other than a brief mention in the *History of Salem, N.H.* (1907) by Edgar Gilbert, there is no mention of Mystery Hill in print until the *Haverhill Evening Gazette* of 1934.

Considering that Munn's later visit encountered Goodwin's fence around the hilltop acre he had purchased but the first visit did not, it is curious that his memories of the trip do not specifically note the fence as a later addition. This may indicate that Munn never actually visited the Mystery Hill site with Lovecraft at all, and that he has confused a visit to the stone ruins at Dogtown with Lovecraft with a visit to the stone ruins at Mystery Hill after Lovecraft's death.

The only other possibility is that Lovecraft first took Munn to the site, having previously visited it himself. Lovecraft returned to Boston's North End in 1927 with Donald Wandrei, who asked to see the house and neighborhood that were the inspiration for Lovecraft's "Pickman's Model," only to discover that the buildings had been demolished between the writing of the story and its appearance in *Weird Tales* in October 1927.[17] If Munn had asked about parts of "The Dunwich Horror" that he didn't recognize from his visits around Athol and Wilbraham, Lovecraft may have offered to show him the site. In such a case, Munn may simply not have recalled the specifics of how he and Lovecraft accessed the site, with or without a fence.

Obviously, for such a scenario, Lovecraft must have visited North Salem before "The Dunwich Horror" was written, and the visit would have to be unmentioned in his surviving correspondence. There is such a combination—8 June 1921, the first day of his visit to Myrta Little. The second day of the visit is the well-documented "Haverhill Convention," but the first day is barely mentioned.

The Little homestead is less than five miles from Mystery Hill along Route 111. The Littles had a car and had taken side trips with Lovecraft. Arriving at the site, Lovecraft would have viewed the ruins atop the hill, seemingly centered on the 4½-ton sacrificial slab. Although it was later determined to be elevated on legs, the table appeared flush with the ground because of centuries of soil accumulation. The Littles would have been well-versed in local lore about Pattee's Caves, particularly the rumors of skeletal remains found around the site.[18] It is no great stretch of the imagination to transform Mystery Hill's stone ruins and legends into the skull-strewn altar atop Sentinel Hill.

In "The Dunwich Horror," Armitage's group wanders off the main trail to the hilltop. If the Little/Lovecraft entourage, unescorted and unfamiliar with the path, similarly veered off their route and onto one of the lumber roads crisscrossing the hill, they would have encountered the glacial cliffs that ring the site—the perpendicular wooded hill referred to in the story. Lovecraft also refers to using "ancient trees they had to scramble up as if a ladder."[19] The research staff at Mystery Hill/America's Stonehenge can testify to the need to use trees in this fashion while navigating around the cliffs.

Seven years later, as Lovecraft was writing "The Dunwich Horror," he took time to drop a note to Myrta Little Davies. Myrta is not mentioned in Lovecraft's correspondence after her marriage, suggesting that contact had tapered off as her life became more oriented on family and her writing career. The fact that Lovecraft chose to send her a letter at the same time as he was writing "The Dunwich Horror" could be a coincidence.[20] Or he may have been recalling a trip with a former peer that took place seventeen years before, which would make the sacrificial table at Mystery Hill a possible inspiration for the stone altar atop Sentinel Hill in Dunwich.

By 1938, William Goodwin had catapulted Pattee's Caves into the national spotlight by suggesting that it was a ninth-century Irish Culdee monastery. A great deal of publicity was generated that stressed the Irish Catholicism of the Culdee monk theory, particularly in 1938–40; as late as 1950, such periodicals as the *Catholic Digest* were still publishing articles on the Irish monks.[21] Munn, Lovecraft bemusedly noted to Barlow, had converted to Catholicism after his marriage.[22] This suggests that the ruins of an ancient Catholic monastery could easily prompt another visit from Munn and his wife. This trip resulted in the incident with caretaker Anna Abbotson that became the predominant memory of the trips. Once through the locked gated, Munn, like Lovecraft before him, found creative inspiration among the ruins.[23]

The Old South Church, Newburyport.

Appendix H
SITES OPEN TO THE PUBLIC

Amesbury, Massachusetts
Amesbury Middle School
220 Main Street

Near the Middle School on Main Street is "The Captain's Well," immortalized in a poem of that name by John Greenleaf Whittier (1807–1892). Lovecraft notes that the well was among his stops in his afternoon tour of Amesbury. Whittier's poem was first published in his collection *At Sundown* (1890). When Whittier wrote the poem in 1889, a nearby town pumping station had drained the spring that fed the well. In the late 1890s, in deference to Whittier tourism, the well was connected to the town water system. Today, a permanent monument engraved with Whittier's poem replaces the rustic original.

John Greenleaf Whittier Home
86 Friend Street

The Whittier Home is where the noted poet lived and worked from 1836 until his death in 1892. Built c. 1829, the house is furnished as Whittier and his family knew it during the mid- to late 1800s and contains authentic furnishings, personal effects of the family, and garden plantings. It is open Saturdays, May through October. Admission fee.

Union Cemetery
Haverhill Road (between Main Street and Hillside Avenue)

Whittier is interred in the Society of Friends Cemetery, which was absorbed into the Union Cemetery. Whittier is in a family plot along with family members commemorated in his most-remembered poem, "Snow Bound." The simple headstone is not hard to find. Ample signage leading to it remains from the Quaker poet's glory days as a literary icon. About 500 feet from Whittier's final resting place is the headstone of Captain Valentine Bagley (1773–1839), the subject of "The Captain's Well."

The grave of John Green Whittier.

Haverhill, Massachusetts

Boardman Street

In "The Shadow out of Time," Professor Nathaniel Wingate Peaslee lived in his ancestral family home on Boardman Street on Golden Hill before he moved to Arkham. Lovecraft and Tryout Smith would have walked up Boardman Street from Groveland Street to reach the scenic vista at the summit of Golden Hill. Sparely inhabited Boardman Street had only two houses that Lovecraft would take note of. The Hazen Garrison is located at 8 Groveland Street, the Mears Farmhouse at 86 Boardman. External view only—both are private residences and not open to the public.

Coombs Building
3 Washington Square

Washington Square is the locus of Haverhill, where the industrial and commercial centers meet. A large brick pedestrian area replaces a stretch of street previously used for parking in front of the Italianate-styled Coombs Building (1860), where trolleys and buses once waited for passengers. At the time of Lovecraft's later visits, the ground floor of the building was Gammon's Drugstore. In Innsmouth, the bus stops in front of Hammond's Drugstore.

Groveland Street

From 1904 to his death in 1948, Charles W. Smith lived at 408 Groveland with only brief interruption. It was there that he printed the *Tryout* on his trusty hand press. The house was destroyed by fire in October 1998, and a new colonial-style house was built in its place. Aside from the street address, the building has no association with Lovecraft or Tryout Smith. Exterior view only—it is a private residence and not open to the public.

Hannah Duston Statue
GAR Park

Formerly in a small green located roughly where Main, Summer, and Winter streets now intersect, the statue stands a short distance away in GAR Park, directly across Main Street from the Library. The green woman on a pedestal pointing with a hatchet is not difficult to find within the park.

Haverhill City Hall
4 Summer Street

The parking lot behind Haverhill's City Hall (along Main Street) is the former site of local manufacturer E. J. M. Hale's home. This house became the YMCA where Lovecraft stayed. Lovecraft did not care for this particular YMCA because the facilities were scattered across the several buildings of the estate. The original Hale/YMCA entrance is marked by the original stone gateposts integrated into the fence along the Main Street side of the parking lot. Formerly the High School, Walter Gilman of "The Dreams in the Witch House" would have attended school there before he went to Miskatonic University.

The home of E. J. M. Hale, purchased by the YMCA in 1897 for its new head-quarters.

Haverhill Country Club
58 Brickett Lane

Lovecraft hypothesized that Haverhill had industrialized at the cost of its colonial neighborhoods, and that the city compensated for that by erecting buildings in medieval styles, specifically Winnekenni Castle and another building he saw under construction, a "Gothic monastery" that would be the new country club's clubhouse. Lovecraft was correct in the Gothic lines, although the finished building was not a monastery but an English Tudor half-timber manor house. The Haverhill Golf and Country Club is still a popular recreation destination atop Brickett Hill where a Tudor building overlooks the links, but it is not the same building that Lovecraft noted. In 1960, the clubhouse was completely gutted by fire. It was rebuilt with the express intention of giving the new building an exterior evocative of the original building's Tudor styling.

Haverhill Historical Society—Buttonwoods Museum
240 Water Street

The Buttonwoods is a Federal style house, built in 1814 as a wedding gift for Samuel White Duncan by his father. It was donated to the historical society by his descendants and opened as a museum on 30 January 1904, with local historian Leonard Woodman Smith as curator. Lovecraft was impressed with both the aristocratic curator and the collection itself, which he felt reflected the original Duncan family rather than an arbitrarily combined exhibit of pieces without relationship to each other. Admission fee.

Haverhill Historical Society—John Ward House
240 Water Street

At the time of Lovecraft's visit, the small house on the grounds of the Historical Society was thought to date back to the very founding of Haverhill as the home of Haverhill's first minister, John Ward. It has subsequently been determined that the wooden-framed building was not as old as believed and dates only to 1720. But Lovecraft sounded positively giddy when he wrote his aunt about the oldest house he had ever seen, let alone entered.

Haverhill Public Library
99 Main Street

The library that Lovecraft visited to read Timothy Dexter's booklet was located on Summer Street. The current building is a larger if inelegant replacement. The third floor of the building is home to Special Collections, where several copies of Tryout Smith's earlier amateur journal, the *Monthly Visitor,* are archived. It is also home to copies of Timothy Dexter's booklet and a peerless collection of local history, photographs, and genealogical sources. The parking lot is shared by the District Court and fills up quickly. Parking on Summer Street is an alternative, as is the parking area behind City Hall.

Hilldale Cemetery
337 Hilldale Avenue

The cemetery on Hilldale Avenue at one time was the grandest and most active cemetery in the city. The condition of the city-run cemetery has rendered plot maps useless, because the paths are now overrun with brush and indiscernible from the weed-choked fields. Most of the headstones are toppled, broken, and vandalized, but a fortunate few are merely buried under years of brush. Although volunteers are addressing years of shameful neglect, the only stone still standing to mark Tryout Smith's final resting place is a Civil War marker for his father Daniel who shares the same plot. That stone's survival is itself a remarkable stroke of fortune. Tryout's daughter Susan and her husband Charles Britton have a family plot nearby. The headstone for Charles and Susan is flush with the ground, the only detectible marker of a plot with at least six other family interments.

Pentucket Burial Ground
Water Street

Established in 1668, the Pentucket was the first burying ground of Haverhill and is the final resting place of the city's earliest inhabitants, many of whom still have headstones. Stones of note here include Nathaniel Peaslee, John Keezar, and Nathaniel Saltonstall. Because the burying ground abuts Linwood Cemetery, it is recommended to avoid parking in front of the cemetery on Water Street and instead to enter Linwood on Mill Street and park along the chain link fence that separates it from Pentucket. (There is a back entrance into Pentucket through the fence.)

Washington Street

The shoe factories of Washington Street and another ten acres of buildings were destroyed by a fire in February 1882. By October, most of the street had been rebuilt, giving rise to a street lined with Queen Anne panel-brick design industrial architecture. In 1976, the area was placed on the National Register of Historic Places as one of the finest examples of such in America, and it remains unchanged to this day. Arriving by train, Lovecraft would leave Railroad Square and find himself at the start of Washington Street. Retail at street level, shoe industry on upper floors, the street was (and is) lined with brick buildings, similar but with the individual touches and varied façades typical of the Queen Anne style. Because of the street's proximity to the railroad station, Lovecraft surely was familiar with the street. His ongoing search for *Old Farmer's Almanacks* must have enticed him to stroll down the street to the bookstores on Washington and Merrimack streets while proceeding to the electric trolleys in Washington Square.

Water Street Fire Station
131 Water Street

Lovecraft's letters note his concern for Tryout Smith during the 1936 flood. That concern was justified; the river crested at thirty feet, and Smith's Groveland Street home narrowly missed inundation. A small disc marking the high water crest is on the outside of the station on the wall facing the river.

Whittier Birthplace
305 Whittier Road, off Route 110

The birthplace of John Greenleaf Whittier was built in 1688 by Thomas Whittier. The house was home to five generations of Whittiers before the birth of the Quaker poet and abolitionist on December 17, 1807. Lovecraft mentions passing the site several times on the trolley heading to Merrimac and Amesbury. He never specifically stated he had visited the house, but a letter to Helen Sully in 1933 suggests he may have. Open seasonally. Admission fee.

Winnekenni Castle

347 Kenoza Avenue (Winnekenni Park)

The Winnekenni Park Conservation Area (700+ acres), overlooking Kenoza Lake, is home to the castle. It was built for Dr. James Nichols, a horticulturist and chemist, who had purchased the Darling Farm, which was on the hill where the castle now stands. Dr. Nichols used the castle not only as a summer home but also as a place to field-test his experiments in chemical fertilizers. Today, Winnekenni Castle is the center of a conservation woodland with nine miles of walking trails that ring the castle.

Merrimac, Massachusetts

Little & Larkin Block

Merrimac Square

The Little & Larkin building was built in 1882 to house carriage finding businesses, specialized companies that supplied the decorative trimmings and peripheral items for the town's major industry—carriage making. The advent of the automobile eliminated the industry,

The Little & Larkin building (1882).

and Edgar J. Davis's father Herman purchased the building in 1916 to open a hardware business that also served as his business headquarters for his chain of stores. When Edgar Davis opened his law offices, they were above his father's store.

Old Sawyer House
20 East Main Street

The Old Sawyer House is a classic New England Colonial house with a centrally located large chimney and unpainted clapboards. The rear slope of the gable roof extends out to create the classic "salt box" shape. Built c. 1735, the museum features local historic artifacts, including furniture and a loom that dates to c. 1675. Lovecraft toured the house with Edgar Davis during his first visit to Merrimac in 1921. It is open occasionally to the public.

West Main Street

The Davis family home was at 16 West Main. The family moved to Merrimac from Haverhill in 1917. It was there that Edgar and his sister Ada, under the tutelage of their mother, a former schoolteacher, blossomed academically into a Harvard-educated lawyer and a noted family physician. It was also here that Lovecraft stayed while visiting the Davises. Exterior view only—the Italianate house is a private residence, not open to the public.

Newbury, Massachusetts
Old Town Hill Reservation
Newman Road

In 1927, on a trip to Newburyport, Lovecraft took a side trip to the Parker River, where he climbed a hill and took in an impressive New England view. This hill is the focus of the 531-acre of Old Town Hill Reservation. The panoramic views include the Great Marsh and New Hampshire's Isles of Shoals. In "The Shadow over Innsmouth," Robert

Olmstead mentions passing the landmark before leaving the main highway on the Innsmouth bus. The reservation is open all year round.

Newburyport, Massachusetts

Atkinson Common
High Street at Moseley Avenue

On 31 August 1932, Lovecraft and W. Paul Cook arrived in Newburyport to view the solar eclipse. Lovecraft's previous explorations of Newburyport provided him with the ideal spot—the open spaces of Atkinson Common.

Postcard showing the open spaces of Newburyport's Atkinson Common.

Dexter-Jackson House
201 High Street

The classic Georgian-style Jackson-Dexter House was built in 1771 and sold to Lord Timothy Dexter in 1798. One of the wealthiest and most eccentric citizens of Newburyport, he added statues on pedestals to the

front of the house and
added a cupola to the roof,
topped with a gilded eagle.
Today, the cupola is the
only remaining modification
made by Dexter. Exterior
view only—it is a private
residence and not open to
the public.

The home of "Lord" Timothy Dexter in
Newburyport as it looks today.

The Historical Society of Old Newbury
98 High Street

The Historical Society of Old Newbury was founded in 1877 as the
Historical and Antiquarian Society. It is located at the Caleb Cushing
House, built in 1808 in the Federal style. On exhibit in the basement is
"The Landlocked Lady," a ship's figurehead that never actually went to
sea. Open seasonally. Admission fee.

Joppa
Water Street

The section of the river bank from Bromfield Street to Ocean Street was
settled by fishermen who, with pious optimism, called the area Joppa,
after the principal seaport of Judea. By the time of Lovecraft's visits,
clamming had replaced fishing as the major industry in Joppa, leading to
a row of clam shacks along the river where it parallels Water Street. The
picture of crowded, weathered shacks, threatening to slide into the river,

is particularly evocative of Innsmouth. In 2009, the last remaining clam shack was transformed into a private residence at 269 Water Street.

Market Square
State Street at Water and Merrimack Streets

Market Square is a tourist destination and thriving business center. At the time of Lovecraft's visits, the location was not even remotely upscale—the buildings were primarily commercial, and various trolley lines converged in the square. Lovecraft notes in a letter than he and Edgar Davis actually passed through Market Square, thinking it was some minor cluster of commercial buildings on the outskirts of town, not the heart of the downtown.

Merrimack Street
Spofford Street to Market Square

Lovecraft's first visit to Newburyport was in 1923 with Edgar Davis. The trolley from Amesbury carried him along Merrimac Street, where the few remaining shipyards and docks lay abandoned and rotting in the wake of the decline in maritime trade. First impressions are lasting impressions, and this sense of abandonment and decay would be an underlying description of Innsmouth. Today, little remains of the industry that once lined the banks, although a visitor might, at low tide, see the occasional orphaned piling poking up out of the water.

Newburyport MBTA Train Station
25 Boston Way

In Lovecraft's day, the train station was on Winter Street. The station is now on Boston Way, off Parker Street. It was constructed in the late 1990s to great fanfare but rapidly became an underused white elephant. Although constructed specifically for the Newburyport extension of a MBTA Commuter Rail line, it has a Lovecraftian connection—the building incorporates the brownstone arches salvaged from the YMCA on State Street that had been destroyed in a fire in 1987.

Newburyport Public Library

94 State Street

The current entrance to the Newburyport Library.

In "The Shadow over Innsmouth," Robert Olmstead spends part of an evening at the library looking up data about Innsmouth. His lack of success only piques his interest even more. Today, the histories of Essex County through which Olmstead, and undoubtedly Lovecraft himself, paged are housed in the Newburyport Archival Center within the library, part of an extensive collection that focuses on genealogy and local history. Built in 1771 for the Tracy family, it was later owned by Timothy Dexter. It became the public library in 1865. The entrance to the library is part of the expansion that occurred following destruction of the YMCA next door in 1987.

Old South Church

29 Federal Street

In a letter to Helen V. Sully of September 1933, Lovecraft agrees with her assessment of Newburyport after her recent visit and hopes that she had time to visit some of the local sites, including the "old church where George Whitefield is buried." A plaster cast of Whitefield's skull now rests atop a plaster replica of his Bible in the alcove that marks his burial. The church offers tours of the interior.

The Old Hill Burying Ground

Auburn Street

The location of the Old Hill Burying Ground (founded in 1729) off High Street between Auburn and Greenleaf streets makes it the most likely of the Newburyport cemeteries for Lovecraft to have visited with Helen Sully. Even if he had not visited it with Sully, he undoubtedly would have stopped there to pay his respects to the cemetery's most famous citizen, Lord Timothy Dexter.

Pettingill-Fowler House
180 High Street

At the time of Lovecraft's visits, The Historical Society of Old Newbury was located in the Pettingill-Fowler House, built in the Federal style with a double hipped roof normally found on Newburyport's Georgian-style houses. It was there that Robert Olmstead viewed the strangely compelling golden jewelry of Innsmouth. The late Georgian building was built in 1792. Exterior view only—it is a private residence and not open to the public.

The Pettingill-Fowler House (1792), home of the Historical Society of Old Newbury at the time of Lovecraft's visits.

Plum Island

Plum Island is a barrier island roughly eight miles long off the coasts of Newburyport, Newbury, Rowley, and Ipswich. An area of the island, with public beaches, businesses, and private residences, lies within the boundaries of Newburyport and Newbury, but most of the southern three-quarters of the island is the Parker River National Wildlife Refuge. The island is accessed by a road running from Newburyport on a causeway. As Robert Olmstead rides the bus to Innsmouth from Newburyport, Plum Island in the distance is the last pleasant vista he sees before entering Innsmouth.

St. Paul's Episcopal Church
166 High Street

Founded in 1711 as an Anglican missionary outpost in the wilds of

British America during the reign of Queen Anne, St. Paul's is the oldest continuously operating Episcopal parish in Massachusetts. The current building was built on the site of the previous church, which was destroyed by fire in 1920. On his first visit to Newburyport in 1923 with Edgar Davis, Lovecraft stopped to observe the new steeple being erected. The cemetery surrounding the property includes several of Davis's relatives.

State Street at Market Square

In "The Shadow over Innsmouth," Robert Olmstead is told that a less expensive alternative to the Arkham train is the Innsmouth bus, which uses Hammond's Drug Store on the square as the Newburyport station. Buses actually departed from Market Square, but tickets were sold at the Ideal Grill at 5 State Street and Market Square. The Ideal Grill does appear in the story, not as the ticket agency but as a handy refuge from the odious vehicle from Innsmouth.

Hampstead, New Hampshire

Lakeview Cemetery
Kent Farm Road

Lakeview Cemetery is the final resting place of Myrta Alice Little Davies (1888–1967), interred in a family plot with her parents Albert and Abbie Little, her husband Arthur Davies, her son Robert Davies, and her sister Edith Lewis.

Little Farmstead
108 East Road

Myrta Little was born and raised in her family's ancestral home on East Road. The house can be traced to Daniel Little, who arrived in Hampstead in 1733, sixteen years before it became a separate community. Exterior view only—it is a private residence and not open to the public.

North Salem, New Hampshire
America's Stonehenge
105 Haverhill Road

In Lovecraft's time, the location was known as Pattee's Caves and consisted of an acre of drywall stone structures centered on a large slab with a groove carved around the edge. When it opened to the public as Mystery Hill in 1959, the slab had been excavated to reveal it was a table. Now known as America's Stonehenge, it includes a vast line of standing stones with solar, lunar and stellar alignments dating to 2000 BCE. Open year round with access restrictions. Check before making plans. Admission fee.

Plaistow, New Hampshire
Maplewood/North Parish Cemetery
23 Atkinson Depot Road

Maplewood/North Parish Cemetery straddles the Haverhill, Massachusetts/Plaistow, New Hamsphire line. Those on the Haverhill side refer the location as the North Parish Cemetery. Among the burials, including some dating back to Haverhill's earliest days, is the Davis family plot, which includes Lovecraft's correspondent and final president of the Daas-Hoffman UAPA, Edgar Jacobs Davis, his parents, and most recently (1991), his sister Dr. Ada Frances Davis. The lot was purchased in 1911 when Edgar's one-year-old sister Ruth died of pneumonia after the local doctor refused to make a house call at 3 AM. The infant's death inspired Ada to join the medical profession. Although the family lived in Merrimac after 1917, it previously dwelt on Rosedale Avenue in Haverhill, barely a half-mile from the state line and the cemetery.

NOTES

Chapter 1: Transformations

1. See Joshi, *H. P. Lovecraft in the* Argosy, for highlights from the war of words.

2. See *The Conservative: Complete 1915–1923*.

3. For more on the adversarial relationship between the two factions, see Faig's "Gidlow Versus Lovecraft."

4. "'Tryout' Smith's Autobiography," 3.

5. This publication premiered the work of James F. Morton (1870–1941), who would later cross swords with HPL in the *Tryout* before becoming one of HPL's most prolific and diverse correspondents.

6. *Boston Daily Globe* (24 February 1899): 12.

7. Currier was a paper box manufacturer and dealer in wooden boxes. He shut down the former Smith operation in 1911.

8. Smith may have helped to pay for the purchase of 408 Groveland Street. The newlywed Brittons lived with Smith at Auburn Street after their marriage in 1898, moving into the new house on Groveland Street in 1901.

9. The term is already in common usage by 1923, based on a reference in a letter to Samuel Loveman. See *Letters to Samuel Loveman and Vincent Starrett*, 17 (cited hereafter as *Loveman/Starrett*).

10. *Selected Letters* 1.140 (cited hereafter as *SL*) and *Letters to Rheinhart Kleiner*, 207–8 (cited hereafter as *Kleiner*).

11. *Collected Essays, Volume 1: Amateur Journalism*, 289–91 (cited hereafter as *CE*).

12. The shed was demolished by a subsequent owner after the property left the Britton family in 1968. The house itself was destroyed by fire in October 1998 and a new colonial-style house built in its place.

Other than the street address, the current building has no association with HPL or Tryout Smith.

13. *SL* 1.298.

Chapter 2: 1921—First Visits

1. "Letter to Myrta Alice Little," *Lovecraft Studies* No. 26 (Spring 1992): 26–30 (cited hereafter as *LS* 26).

2. *I Am Providence: The Life and Times of H. P. Lovecraft,* 1.315.

3. *United Amateur* (November 1920). Reprinted in *CE* 1.265.

4. *SL* 1.139 and *Kleiner,* 207.

5. Faig, "Lovecraft's 1937 Diary."

6. Waiting for the train at Westville at the end of his second trip to Hampstead in August, HPL posted a letter to his aunt from Westville. *SL* 1.148.

7. *SL* 1.184.

8. The article appeared in the *Tryout* for July 1921 and has been reprinted in *CE* 1.289–91 and *Writings in the* Tryout, 50–52. See Appendix A.

9. *Kleiner,* 207–8.

10. *Kleiner,* 112.

11. "The Terrible Old Man" contains the first mention of Kingsport, one of HPL's fictional towns. HPL subsequently would correlate Kingsport with Marblehead, Massachusetts.

12. Probably "Tryout's Lament for the Vanished Spider," in the *Tryout,* January 1920. The cat would be eulogized the following year by HPL in "Sir Thomas Tryout: Died November 15, 1921" [as by Ward Phillips], *Tryout,* December 1921. Reprinted in *The Ancient Track,* 147–48.

13. *Letters to Alfred Galpin,* 101–2 (cited hereafter as *Galpin*).

14. Winnekenni Castle and surrounding property were sold to the City of Haverhill in 1895 and was placed under the supervision of the Water Department. It was used for social gatherings and civic events until about 1920 when interest waned.

15. *SL* 1.148.

16. Although "The Outsider" remains one of HPL's most commonly reprinted works, HPL later regarded it verbose and overly elaborate, and although not without merit, a blatant imitation of Poe. *SL* 3.378–79.

17. *SL* 1.148.

18. "The Pinnacle" has not appeared on USGS maps for more than a century. The name itself dates to 1721 when lands were granted to Lemuel Tucker including the "Pinnacle," which bordered on the "Twelve Rod Way," a road originally laid out in 1663.

19. *Essential Solitude: The Letters of H. P. Lovecraft and August Derleth,* 2.769 (cited hereafter as *Derleth*). HPL identified his planisphere as a Barritt-Serviss Star and Planet Finder. First released in the mid-1900s, it claimed to be "The Only Practical Combination Star, Planet and Sun and Moon Map" and consisted of a 15-inch diameter disc showing constellations, ecliptic with raised planets, and Gregorian and Zodiacal calendars.

20. *Galpin,* 102.

21. *United Amateur* (March 1921). Reprinted in *CE* 1.314.

22. *Loveman/Starrett,* 20

23. *Letters from New York,* 22.

24. *SL* 1.289.

25. See *SL* 3.16–17, 25, 363–64 for HPL's somewhat limited work on the Phillips family. Kenneth W. Faig, Jr., has reviewed HPL's tree and suggests that HPL's primary source probably was *Phillips Genealogies* (1885) by Albert M. Phillips. HPL traces his line back to a Michael Phillips of Newport, RI, whom HPL identifies as a son of Reverend George Phillips. However, the Phillips book is not the source of this erroneous connection between Michael and Reverend George. Someone in the family may have hired a genealogist, who, typically for the period, was inclined to find desired connections rather than documented ones.

Chapter 3: Whittierland and Newburyport

1. *LS* 26: 28.

2. The house was located near the intersection of Main Street on Westville Road. It may not be a coincidence that one of his neighbors was Vladimir Sikorsky, a physician specializing in nervous conditions. Dr. Sikorsky also ran a private hospital at his Main Street property.

3. *SL* 1.218–24.

4. *Loveman/Starrett,* 20.

5. *Kleiner,* 30, 65.

6. *The Annotated Supernatural Horror in Literature*, 52.

7. *Elsie Venner: A Romance of Destiny*, 1.28–29.

8. *Loveman/Starrett*, 20; *Kleiner*, 230.

9. The existing span, completed in 1910, was designed to resemble the chain bridge of 1810 that it replaced. Although the new bridge is suspended with cables, it is referred to as the "Chain Bridge."

10. *Galpin*, 246; *Loveman/Starrett*, 20.

11. Harriet Prescott Spofford (1835–1921) played hostess to such New England literary figures as Emerson, Holmes, Whittier, and Lowell. Deer Island was where Spofford wrote most of her works, including a scant few tales of supernatural, madness, and obsession such as the haunted railroad engineer in "The Black Bess" *(Galaxy,* May 1868), a living portrait gallery in "The Godmothers" (*Cosmopolitan,* March 1896), the vampiric "The Conquering Will" (*Smart Set,* June 1901), and the first haunted automobile tale, "The Mad Lady" (*Scribner's,* February 1916). Most of Deer Island is now town-owned conservation land, but the Spofford house remains, still a private residence.

12. "Supernatural Horror in Literature" was published in 1927 in W. Paul Cook's amateur press venture, the *Recluse.* HPL revised it for reissue in the *Fantasy Fan* (October 1933–January 1935). Both versions have been reprinted. *The Annotated Supernatural Horror in Literature* (2000; rev. 2012), with extensive textual and bibliographic notes, is the recommended text.

13. HPL to Richard Ely Morse, 26 January 1935 (ms., John Hay Library).

14. Haverhill may have played a part in the Marsh refinery's evolution. The trolley to Smith's home from Haverhill's downtown branched off Water Street onto Groveland Street. As the trolley turned left onto Groveland Street, to the right, the Haverhill Paperboard mill would be seen across the river. Erected in 1902, the mill would have been visible rising above the trees on the opposite shore in apparent isolation. It was demolished in 2012.

15. *Loveman/Starrett*, 20. HPL echoes the description in *Galpin,* 146, attributing the epithet "City of the Dead" to John Quincy Adams.

16. Drake, *New England Legends and Folk-Lore,* 292–301. One of Dexter's statues, the statue of William Pitt, survives at the Historical Society of Old Newbury, on loan from the Smithsonian.

17. *SL* 4.259–60.

18. *Galpin,* 150.

19. *Galpin,* 152.

20. *Galpin,* 149–50. The 1838 edition of *A Pickle for the Knowing Ones,* a facsimile of the second edition of 1805, remains in print to this day. Written in a phonetic orthography that borders on unreadability, the prose was further complicated by a total lack of punctuation. When readers complained about the lack of punctuation, Dexter reprinted the booklet with a page of assorted punctuation marks at the end so that readers could "peper and solt it as they plese."

21. "Humphrey Repton, Landscape Gardener, 1752–1818." HPL minimally sent copies of the bulletin to Galpin (Galpin, 152), Kleiner (*Kleiner,* 230), and Frank Belknap Long.

22. *Letters to James F. Morton,* 45 (cited hereafter as *Morton*).

23. *SL* 1.243–44.

Chapter 4: Intermezzo (1924–26)

1. *Letters from New York,* 155.

2. HPL to Maurice Moe, 15 June 1925 (ms., Brown University). Excerpt quoted in Joshi, *I Am Providence,* 2.586–87.

3. *I Am Providence,* 2.587.

4. *SL* 2.26.

5. In *An H. P. Lovecraft Encyclopedia,* Joshi and Schultz cite the unpublished letter dated 2 December 1925, at Brown University's John Hay library. When "The Loved Dead," co-written by HPL, appeared in the May–June–July 1924 issue of *Weird Tales,* authorities in Indiana attempted to ban the entire issue.

6. The colonial Pentucket burying ground has no vault. Hilldale Cemetery, where Tryout's family was buried, and the newly opened Linwood Cemetery, within walking distance of Groveland Street, have vaults, but they are too small.

7. *Morton,* 72; excerpt in *SL* 1.326. *Ardinii Varini* is Lovecraft's Latinization of the name Warren Harding. President Warren G. Harding had died in August 1923, and a two-cent memorial stamp was issued in September. The stamp was scheduled to be sold for 60 days, but demand was so great that the Post Office made the stamp available

through February 1924. The presses used for the stamp were unable to meet demand, necessitating a second type of press (rotary vs. flat plate) to supplement the printing. A subtle but distinct difference between the two types of printing created a variation considered desirable by collectors such as Tryout Smith.

8. The Maplewood Cemetery lot was purchased in 1911 when Edgar's family lived on Main Street in Haverhill, near the Plaistow state line. Edgar's one-year-old sister Ruth died of pneumonia after the local doctor refused to make a house call at 3 AM. The family moved from Haverhill to Merrimac, MA, in 1917.

9. *Lord Timothy Dexter of Newburyport, Massachusetts* (1925) was Marquand's first literarily significant book. Best known for his "Mr. Moto" stories, Marquand's mainstream fiction, even if less lucrative than his pulp fiction, garnered him much respect. One of Marquand's recurring themes was the restrictions to life among America's bluebloods and the risks of those who aspired to join the elite, making Dexter an obvious topic.

10. *The Ancient Track,* 320.

11. The tunnels exist, but the theories surrounding their origins, number, and routes have achieved legendary status. Since most of the entrances were sealed long ago and located in the basement of private homes, access has not allowed a study of the brick-lined tunnels, large enough for a man to walk upright. Current theories are that they were built by merchants to transport contraband and circumvent the Embargo Act of 1807, or to serve as a system to direct water to locations in the city in case of fire.

12. *Derleth,* 1.51, 52.

13. See Appendix C.

14. *The Ancient Track,* 323.

Chapter 5: Innsmouth Ascendant (1927–31)

1. *Galpin,* 125. As noted in Chapter 2, the building was not as old as originally believed.

2. "The Trip of Theobald" first appeared in the *Tryout* (September 1927). Reprinted in *CE* 4.11–12.

3. HPL and Donald Wandrei, *Mysteries of Time and Spirit*, 156–57 (cited hereafter as *Wandrei*).

4. "The Trip of Theobald," *CE* 4.11.

5. *Wandrei*, 161.

6. The text written in Haverhill, obviously rushed and coupled with the ever-present tryoutisms in the published version, is somewhat difficult to follow at points. In his notes on the essay in *CE* 4, S. T. Joshi uncharitably says the first half of the text is "incoherent." The second half, done at a more leisurely pace, is more in HPL's normal style.

7. *SL* 2.175.

8. The earliest suggestion of a visit to Salem, NH, by HPL appears to be a passing reference by Andrew E. Rothovius in an article published in *Yankee* magazine. This casual thought resulted in his "Lovecraft and the New England Megaliths" for *The Dark Brotherhood and Other Pieces*. See Appendix G for the author's stance on the debate.

9. HPL never signed the final divorce decree, although Sonia believed he did. Faig notes that in addition to making Sonia's marriage in 1936 bigamous, it complicated HPL's literary estate.

10. *Miscellaneous Writings*, 512. The original letter appeared in the Providence paper on 20 March 1929.

11. The lengthy travelogue was never intended for publication and probably was too long to be marketed. L. Sprague de Camp rediscovered the manuscript in the mid-1970s while working on his biography of HPL. He published it in *To Quebec and the Stars*. The reference to Hannah Duston is on 157–58 (also in *CE* 4.134).

12. *Derleth*, 1.387, 390.

13. Postcard from HPL and Cook to Clark Ashton Smith, postmarked Boston, October 5, 1931. Privately owned.

14. *Wandrei*, 287. The *Recluse* was the name of Cook's most recent amateur journal.

15. See HPL to Strauch, 5 November 1931: "I visited four of my favourite ancient towns—Portsmouth, N.H., & Newburyport, Salem & Marblehead, Mass. Portsmouth & Newburyport are almost solidly archaic . . ." In "Letters to Carl Ferdinand Strauch," *Lovecraft Annual* No. 4 (2010): 57.

16. Robert Olmstead is not named in the finished story, but his name appears in surviving work notes. The notes are included in the 1994 annotated edition of *The Shadow over Innsmouth*.

17. The B&M train station was located on Winter Street opposite Pleasant Street. The building was destroyed by fire in 1968 and the train corridor abandoned soon after. The old train corridor is now a "rail to trail" project, paralleling the north side of Route 1 from the new MBTA train station to the Merrimack River.

18. *The H. P. Lovecraft Companion*, 92–94.

19. The hill is the focal point of the 531-acre of Old Town Hill Reservation. It is owned and managed by The Trustees of Reservation, a member-supported, nonprofit conservation organization.

20. Caitlín R. Kiernan, whose recurring Snow Family has a house at the mouth of the Manuxet, believes HPL shortened the length of Plum Island. She places Innsmouth Harbor at the mouth of the Castle Neck River at Crane Beach.

21. *Derleth*, 1.411; *Fritz Leiber and H. P. Lovecraft: Writers of the Dark*, 16; *Letters to Robert Bloch*, 12.

22. *SL* 3.435–36.

23. *Derleth*, 1.429.

Chapter 6: Dreams and Eclipses (1932–33)

1. *SL* 4.91.

2. *Derleth*, 2.483.

3. Smith, *Letters to H. P. Lovecraft*, 34; *A Means to Freedom: The Letters of H. P. Lovecraft and Robert E. Howard*, 1.279 (cited hereafter respectively as *Smith* and *Howard*).

4. These articles have been collected in *First Writings: Pawtuxet Valley Gleaner, 1906*.

5. Letter to Elizabeth Toldridge, *SL* 4.54.

6. *Morton*, 303. He repeats the description, almost verbatim in *Howard*, 1.426.

7. Bossy Gillis's building no longer stands. In 1972, the new drawbridge carrying US-1 across the Merrimack to Salisbury, MA, was named after him.

8. *O. Henry Memorial Award Prize Stories of 1932*, 274, 283.

9. *Derleth*, 2.538.

10. *Derleth*, 2.544. Derleth was concerned that HPL would be offended by going behind his back.

11. *Wandrei*, 318, 319; *Howard*, 2.585; *SL* 4.146. Reaction to the story has always been mixed. Robert E. Howard (*Howard*, 2.612) thought the story quite good. Fritz Leiber was particularly fond of it, as evidenced by his "Through Hyperspace with Brown Jenkin: HPL's Contribution to Speculative Fiction" in *The Dark Brotherhood and Other Pieces* (also reprinted in *Lovecraft Remembered* and *Leiber*). S. T. Joshi, on the other hand, feels HPL "lapses into hackneyed and overblown purple prose that almost sounds like a parody of his own style" (*I Am Providence*, 2.823).

12. "Memories of Lovecraft: II," *Arkham Collector* (Winter 1969), reprinted in *Lovecraft Remembered*.

13. *Lovecraft Remembered*, 278.

14. *SL* 4.259–60.

15. *Howard Phillips Lovecraft: Dreamer on the Nightside*, 192–97.

16. *I Am Providence*, 2.757, 855 dates the trips to Onset as mid-August 1930 and a weekend in late July 1933.

17. *SL* 4.328–29.

Chapter 7: Shadows out of Haverhill (1934–36)

1. *O Fortunate Floridian: H. P. Lovecraft's Letters to R. H. Barlow*, 170 (cited hereafter as *Barlow*). The editors misread the postcard and in their notes claim the meeting itself took place in Lawrence. The message's context clearly indicates all three added their comments at 408 Groveland Street.

2. HPL's "Commonplace Book," item 182 (c. 1930). The rough notes and story ideas have been in print in various editions since 1938. The definitive and annotated edition is *Commonplace Book* (1987), but the text can be found more easily in *Miscellaneous Writings*, 87–103.

3. *SL* 3.217, 4.25–26.

4. "Memories of Lovecraft" is Barlow's journal of HPL's two-month visit in May–June 1934 at his family's home in DeLand, Florida. The full text version first appeared in *On Lovecraft and Life* and has been reprinted in *Barlow* (11 and 402, respectively). HPL named Barlow his

literary executor, much to the irritation of August Derleth and Donald Wandrei.

5. Unfortunately, Nutting neglected to keep a record of modifications. Minimally, he replaced existing square-paned, sash windows with diamond-paned, hinged casement windows to emphasize English medieval manor style he felt was the original look of the house. This would have been appropriate if the house was old as Nutting believed (c. 1680) instead of the actual age of c. 1724.

6. *Dark Brotherhood*, 30–63; reprinted in *CE* 2.

7. Letter to Clark Ashton Smith, *SL* 2.27.

8. *The Writings of Henry David Thoreau*, 11.111.

9. Thoreau, *A Week on the Concord and Merrimack Rivers*, *Writings* 1.341–45; *Journal II*, *Writings* 8.7.

10. Burleson, "Humor Beneath Horror." Burleson also covers the material in *H. P. Lovecraft: A Critical Study*, in consolidated form from the earlier article.

11. "Humour Beneath Horror," 5.

12. *SL* 5.124. He suggests similar thoughts to Emil Petaja (*SL* 5.120) and Clark Ashton Smith (*SL* 5.130).

13. *Wandrei*, 356.

14. Letter to Duane W. Rimel dated 4 August 1935, quoted in *Derleth*, 2.697.

15. *Derleth*, 2.691, 711, 719

16. Wandrei, 24 September 1935.

17. *Barlow*, 294. See also 131, 137, and 224 for other complaints about the typos.

18. *Wandrei*, 368.

19. *Galpin*, 222.

20. *Barlow*, 207–8.

21. *Barlow*, 326–30.

22. *Barlow*, 335.

23. *Barlow*, 373. The number of errors continued to climb.

24. *Wandrei*, 384.

25. *I Am Providence*, 2.999.

Chapter 8: Aftermath

1. Kenneth Faig, Jr., "Lovecraft's 1937 Diary." Faig notes that the term "death diary," although commonly used, is a misnomer. The diary was a commercial-style diary volume for 1937 and HPL began the diary on 1 January. He also completed a section of friends' addresses, making the diary more valuable than just a chronicle of HPL's final days. The diary has been lost but transcriptions Barlow had made for Derleth survive.

2. HPL died on 15 March 1937. *Smith,* 55 is a letter by Smith dated 30 March, responding to Derleth's book idea, already in the planning stages.

3. See George T. Wetzel's *The Lovecraft Scholar* for his research into the copyright mess. Wetzel's conclusions suggest Derleth never controlled the rights and most of HPL's works have fallen into the public domain as a result of his interference.

4. *Weird Tales* did not own the rights to the later stories and the agreement with the Gamwell heirs was not binding under the 1909 copyright law, which assigned the rights to the widow. Since Sonia did not realize until the late 1960s that she was HPL's widow, she had not renewed copyrights that would have prevented HPL's works from entering the public domain.

5. "A Plea for Lovecraft" originally appeared in the *Ghost* No. 3 (May 1945). It is reprinted in *LS* 19/20 and *W. Paul Cook: The Wandering Life of a Yankee Printer.*

6. HPL made the declaration in letters to James F. Morton and his aunt Lillian Clark as his time in New York was coming to an end. It is a widely reprinted remark. The Morton letter is in *Morton,* 93. *SL* 2.51 contains excerpts. The letter to Clark, which reflects HPL's desperate need to return to Providence, can be found in *Letters from New York,* 289 with excerpts in de Camp, 258, *I Am Providence,* 1.391, and most of the collections of HPL's letters edited by Joshi and Schultz.

Appendix A: The Haverhill Convention

1. Excerpt from "Ode to Solitude" by Alexander Pope.

2. Opening lines of the first *Eclogue* of Virgil, where Tityrus is encountered relaxing beneath a beech tree.

Appendix B: First Impressions of Newburyport

1. The entire letter is reproduced in *Loveman/Starrett*, 16–23. The annotated edition of *The Shadow over Innsmouth* (1994) includes an excerpt in the introductory notes, pp. 8–9.

2. Author/lecturer and pop psychiatrist David Van Bush was HPL's least liked revision client. Like Dexter, he came from humble, rural origins. See HPL's condescending description of Bush in his letter to Anne Tillery Renshaw in *SL* 1.185–86.

3. Pegāna is the dwelling place of the pantheon of gods created by Irish fantasist Lord Dunsany.

Appendix C: Tryout's Return to Haverhill

1. "Old Haunts" by Martin Farquhar Tupper.

2. "Town" by Martin Farquhar Tupper.

Appendix E: Howard Prescott Lovecraft

1. Edward Young, *Night Thought V,* l. 1011: "Death loves a shining mark, a signal blow."

Appendix G: H. P. Lovecraft, "The Dunwich Horror," and Mystery Hill

1. "More on the Great Stone Mysteries," 168.

2. *Dark Brotherhood*, 187–88. Rothovius was of the opinion that the slabs stones were not pre-Columbian and were actually artifacts from a colonial smelting operation that created counterfeit silver and gold coins.

3. *The H. P. Lovecraft Companion,* 59. Shreffler also notes the guide was quite insistent that the slab was the base of a cider press.

4. The Pelham origin is similar to a documented story of a stone slab now held by the Museum Village at Old Smith's Clove in Monroe, NY. Antique collector Roscoe W. Smith had purchased a cider press in Vermont for his collection in 1938, but the wooden base had rotted away. He learned of a stone base in a cellar hole in Pelham and was able to purchase it prior to the Quabbin flooding and had it shipped to New York, where he cobbled it together for his cider mill exhibit. Similarly, Goshen is home to a mysterious drywall masonry tunnel, but there is no record of a slab in the area.

5. W. H. Pugmire, correspondence with the author, 20 July 2012.

6. H. Warner Munn, letters to Donald Burleson, 7 February and 22 March 1979. Burleson subsequently published a summary of the letters in "H. P. Lovecraft and Mystery Hill."

7. Malcolm Pearson, letter to William B. Goodwin, 24 January 1937; Mystery Hill Archive.

8. Frank Portors, "Problem for Archaeologists," *Haverhill Evening Gazette* (15 August 1934). Portors interviewed Elsie Conley, who embellished a number of points. She was one of numerous local residents who used the location for picnicking and exploration.

9. William B. Goodwin and archaeologist Gary Vescelius were among the guests of the Abbotsons (Goodwin to H. Abbotson, 15 February 1934; Vescelius to H. Abbotson, 4 September 1945; et al., Mystery Hill Archive).

10. *H. P. Lovecraft Companion,* 32.

11. Munn, letter to Burleson, 7 February 1979; Philip Shreffler, letter to the author, 8 November 1987. Shreffler paraphrases Munn as having told how "Howard . . . strode among the stones, talking about how well the setting would suit his mythos demons." This version, though less flamboyant than the book quotation, seems the more reasonable.

12. The article ran in two parts: *Whispers* No. 9 (December 1976) and *Whispers* No. 13/14 (October 1979); rpt. as "H.P.L.: A Reminiscence" in *Lovecraft Remembered* (1998).

13. Today, Dogtown is protected watershed woodlands, known for walking trails, boulders, and abandoned cellar holes. Adding to the ghost town vibe are the "Babson Boulders," a series of 24 inspirational messages carved into the boulders by stonecutters hired by local philanthropist Roger Babson to give them work during the Great Depression.

14. In an interview with Jessica Amanda Salmonson in 1979, Munn notes that when he moved to Tacoma, WA, in 1950, he was not sure if the relocation was permanent. He boarded up the house until the decision was finalized. Five years later, he returned to pack up and sell the house, only to discover the roof over his library had been leaking for several years and most of his collections of early pulp magazines and his correspondence were virtually destroyed by water damage and layers of

mold and mildew. Munn ended up shoveling the collection out a window and burning it.

15. See Burleson, *H. P. Lovecraft: A Critical Study*, 141–45 for more on the Athol-Wilbraham elements in "The Dunwich Horror" gained from these trips to Central Massachusetts.

16. *Wandrei*, 250.

17. *SL* 4.385–86.

18. Unsubstantiated tales persist to this day of Indian skulls being found and removed from the site prior to Goodwin's ownership. Native pottery has been found near the cliffs, but skeletal remains would have disintegrated in the acidic soil long before English colonization of the region. Animal remains and overactive oral traditions are likely the sources of the Mystery Hill skulls.

19. *DH* 191–92.

20. The letter has been lost, but the envelope with a postmark of July 27, 1928, was auctioned to a private collector.

21. "Did the Irish Discover America," *Catholic Digest* (August 1950). The author was Clay Perry, a freelance writer who wrote extensively on the site with varying degrees of enthusiasm and accuracy from 1938 into the 1950s.

22. *Barlow*, 405. "H. Warner Munn has such a belief in the supernatural as to have caused him to become Catholic after his marriage; and almost repudiate his earlier work as morbid and not nice."

23. Munn's *Merlin's Ring* was published in 1974. According to this fantasy, Merlin's godson warns the Culdees of an approaching Viking attack and directs them to a sanctuary in what can be inferred to be the northeast region of North America.

LOVECRAFT: A SENSE OF PLACE AND HIGH STRANGENESS

Chris Perridas

It is a pleasure to write this afterword and endorse the significance of David Goudsward's current contribution to Lovecraft research. His well-known expositions of stones and their mythic importance, notably in New England horror literature, is becoming legendary. Dave and I have had many pleasurable correspondences on the intricacies of Haverhill, Lovecraft, and "Tryout" Smith. That this notable work has now seen print is wonderful, and if you now own this book, know that this is one of those classic "Lovecraft collectibles" you will cherish. If you plan to read the cover off, as I will, you may wish to buy a second copy and keep it in your bookcase as the collectible it shall become.

My goal is to emphasize what David Goudsward has so admirably done in this book: to call out Lovecraft's sense of the weird in geographic place. This is much like a lowly church pastor putting a summation on a famous evangelist's fiery sermon. Haverhill has been too long neglected, and now is rightfully served in the pantheon of Lovecraftian scholarship.

The mature Lovecraft was quite atheistic, but this did not make him immune to a sense of the mythic. In fact, his later fictional career was an attempt to supersede his personal sense of the weird in order to eradicate the mundane Gothic. Virtually his entire waking life was spent trying to find that one essential kernel of the weird within his reading, or during his travels. Some Lovecraftians feel Lovecraft was immune to mythic religiosity. He was not. Lovecraft grew up in a religious environment, and while he rejected the mythic tenets of

Christianity, he attended a type of Sunday School circa 1910 and read many alternative paradigms of religiosity throughout his lifetime. Some of these mythic expositions, such as theosophy and cabalism, he rejected, but he embraced other mythic forms such as anti-Zionism and a type of Aryanism. Scholars have worked hard to uncover what specific set of rose-colored glasses Lovecraft used, and this is especially significant when it comes to his critique of place.

Although Joseph Campbell is today the iconic expert of myth, let us appeal instead to Mircea Eliade to discuss Lovecraft's sense of place. Eliade and other French philosophers of myth felt that geography was not a simple matter of geology, topography, and measurements. The English version of Eliade's *The Sacred and the Profane* appeared in 1957 and has not received attention by Lovecraft scholars. Eliade explained that the mythic can be divided between "sacred," or that which is transcendent; *hierophany,* which is revelatory; and *numinous,* or that which is overwhelming to man. The geographic "place" is not seen by humans as simply a matter of space, but it always has some sociological mythic quality to it.

Let us take a simple passage such as one in "The Trip of Theobald," which can be dated to about 1 September 1927:

> Saturday took a cheap excursion to the White Mountains—saw real mountains for the first time in my life, and had some superb views at Crawford Notch. Ascended Mt. Washington by cog-wheel railway, and had some splendid views on the way up, though it rained just as I reached the summit.

Here, to a general audience, Lovecraft seems pedantic. But is he? Lovecraftians usually focus on his passion for the colonial, and this is not lacking. However, what may be overlooked is the eight times Lovecraft emphasizes the panoramic view from heights. Besides the White Mountains, we read:

> I climbed a high hill west of Athol . . . went up in the observation tower . . . splendid view of the town . . . Portland . . . a beautiful hill city with magnificent views. . . took a side trip . . . to Portland Head

Lighthouse . . . took a side trip to Parker River, climbing a great hill . . . a fine panoramic view from Governor's Hill . . . explored the cliffs of Magnolia.

In addition, while he uses the pejorative "cheap," he subtly mentions that "it rained just as I reached the summit." One might think this is a negative description; but this is not the case. That this event is of mythic importance—through his unique perspective—is testified by a brief exclamation in a postcard to Donald Wandrei dated 27 August 1927. Just as we are deflated by Lovecraft's bland description of the New Hampshire tourist trap, he surprises Wandrei by saying: "Ascended Mt. Washington, but find the mountains slightly lacking in subtlety"; he then slips in a "P.S. Glimpsed The Other Gods!"

By 11 September 1927, Lovecraft had digested his mountaintop experience. It was no longer a routine tourist experience. Recollection was reinforced by Wandrei's effusive discussions of Clark Ashton Smith's otherworldly paintings.

I don't know whether or not you have seen real mountains—I had not, hence the spectacle of these celebrated peaks [the White Mountains] was to me especially impressive. The slopes rose sheer & forbidding as the train stole among them, & as clouds touched the summits I could well imagine the habitancy of strange & Clarcashtonic shapes in those unfrequented altitudes. The view ascending Mt. Washington was beyond imagination—& when near the summit clouds gathered below, leaving one lone & cosmic on the barren pinnacle, across which swept furious winds that are not of earth.

Here in a matter of ten days, Lovecraft went from a serendipitous, touristy experience to "high strangeness." The pivot was likely the conflation of Wandrei's discussion of Smith's paintings with his sorting through the whirlwind experiences of his trip back home in his cloistered room. We can only imagine what his dreams were like.

Dave Goudsward has shown that Lovecraft's experiences with Tryout Smith and in Haverhill were sometimes mundane, sometimes profound. He has shown which unique events were significant enough to be included in Lovecraft's list of mythic experiences, significant enough to be included as underpinnings for his most important fictional works.

Lovecraft was constantly on the lookout for "high strangeness," and these events were fleeting and all but invisible to his closest friends. Thus is the curse of a prophet in his own times.

Take the implied incident that Goudsward explains. Lovecraft visited the Pentucket Burying Ground in Haverhill on Water Street in August 1934. A fleeting glimpse of Nathanael Peaslee's grave not only was indelibly inscribed into Lovecraft's mind, but remained in his mind until used in his next story. The strange mythic element of this incident cannot be overemphasized. An ordinary tourist would have been enamored of visiting Whittier's grave or Whittier's birthplace, but Whittier was "profane" in Lovecraft's viewpoint (and in the terms of Mircea Eliade's thesis). Peaslee, however, was *numinous* to Lovecraft. This is not meant to give any greater intrinsic value between a Haverhill pioneer or a beloved poet, but to point out that Lovecraft danced to an entirely different drumbeat when it came to mythic geography.

Lovecraft clearly was not religious, but that did not stop him from having a missionary zeal. His passion was the weird, and he imposed it on anyone who came within earshot, and "preached" it to every disciple. He made it an essential ingredient in most of his tens of thousands of letters—homilies to the weird. The Peaslee monument became his touchstone in "The Shadow out of Time," and thus became part of his *hierophany:* part of his revelation of the weird.

We do not know why or how this may have connected in such a way to Lovecraft, but there is a possible clue. Goudsward states, "The details regarding Haverhill in "The Shadow out of Time" are as accurate as those regarding Newburyport in "The Shadow over Innsmouth." Before Peaslee secured his position at Miskatonic, he lived in his ancestral family home on Boardman Street on Golden Hill. Rising almost 300 feet above the surrounding area, Golden Hill gives an expansive view of the city and the Merrimack River. The walk to the hilltop's scenic vista would be on Boardman Street, as seen on any of Lovecraft's visits with Tryout Smith." This does not seem to be a coincidence. Graves were psychologically critical to Lovecraft from the time of the burial of his grandmother in 1896. There must have been some overwhelming sensation of the contrast of seeing a panorama to the usually cloistered bookworm, and he subconsciously emphasizes this in his letters whenever he experienced it. Lovecraft could not help but fix in his mind upon the contrast between the atheistic finality of death and the expansiveness of cosmic eternity.

BIBLIOGRAPHY

Architectural Heritage of Haverhill. Virginia Bilmazes Bernard, coordinator. Haverhill, MA: Trustees of the Haverhill Public Library, 1976.

Barlow, R. H. *On Lovecraft and Life.* Ed. S. T. Joshi. West Warwick, RI: Necronomicon Press, 1992.

Burleson, Donald R. *H. P. Lovecraft: Critical Study.* Westport, CT: Greenwood Press, 1983.

———. "Humour Beneath Horror: Some Sources for 'The Dunwich Horror' and 'The Whisperer in Darkness.'" *Lovecraft Studies* No. 2 (Spring 1980): 5–15.

———. "H. P. Lovecraft and Mystery Hill." *NEARA Journal* 14, No. 4 (Spring 1980): 84–86.

———. *Lovecraft: Disturbing the Universe.* Lexington: University Press of Kentucky, 1990.

Cook, W. Paul. *W. Paul Cook: The Wandering Life of a Yankee Printer.* Ed. Sean Donnelly. New York: Hippocampus Press, 2007.

Davis, Sonia H. *The Private Life of H. P. Lovecraft.* Ed. S. T. Joshi. West Warwick, RI: Necronomicon Press, 1985 (rev. ed. 1992).

de Camp, L. Sprague. *Lovecraft: A Biography.* Garden City, NY: Doubleday, 1975.

Dexter, Timothy. *A Pickle for the Knowing Ones.* Newburyport, MA: Historical Society of Old Newbury, 1916 (reprint of 1838 edition).

Doyle, Jean Foley, and Jennifer Karin. *Life in Newburyport, 1900–1950: A Collection of News Events, City Affairs, and Memories from the First Half of the Twentieth Century.* Portsmouth, NH: P. E. Randall, 2007.

Drake, Samuel Adams. *A Book of New England Legends and Folk Lore in Prose and Poetry.* Boston: Roberts Bros., 1884.

Everts, R. Alain. *The Death of a Gentleman: The Last Days of Howard Phillips Lovecraft.* Madison, WI: Strange Co., 1987.

Faig, Kenneth W., Jr. "Gidlow Versus Lovecraft." *Cyaëgha* No. 7 (Autumn 2012): 24–33.

———. "Lovecraft's 1937 Diary." *Lovecraft Annual* No. 6 (2012): 153–78.

———. *The Parents of Howard Phillips Lovecraft.* West Warwick, RI: Necronomicon Press, 1990.

———. "Some Smith Family Notes." *Fossil* 108, No. 4 (July 2012): 16–19.

———. *The Unknown Lovecraft.* New York: Hippocampus Press, 2009.

Goudsward, David. *America's Stonehenge: The Mystery Hill Story from Ice Age to Stone Age.* Boston: Branden Books, 2003.

———. *Ancient Stone Sites of New England and the Debate Over Early European Exploration.* Jefferson, NC: McFarland, 2006.

Hale, Albert. *Old Newburyport Houses.* Boston: W. B. Clarke Co., 1912.

Halpern, Paul and Michael C. LaBossiere. "Mind out of Time: Identity, Perception, and the Fourth Dimension in H. P. Lovecraft's 'The Shadow out of Time' and 'The Dreams in the Witch House.'" *Extrapolation* 50, No. 3 (2009): 512–533.

Holmes, Oliver Wendell. *Elsie Venner: A Romance of Destiny.* Boston: Ticknor & Fields, 1861.

"Humphrey Repton, Landscape Gardener, 1752–1818." *Bulletin of the Haverhill Public Library* 7, No. 24 (April 1923): 97–98.

Joshi, S. T. ed. *H. P. Lovecraft in the* Argosy: *Collected Correspondence from the Munsey Magazines.* West Warwick, RI: Necronomicon Press, 1994.

———. *I Am Providence: The Life and Times of H. P. Lovecraft.* New York: Hippocampus Press, 2010. 2 vols.

Joshi, S. T., and David E. Schultz. *An H. P. Lovecraft Encyclopedia.* 2001. New York: Hippocampus Press, 2004.

Kuntz, Eugene B. *Thoughts and Pictures.* Haverhill, MA: H. P. Loveracft [*sic*] and C. W. Smith, 1932.

Livesey, T. R. "Dispatches from the Providence Observatory: Astronomical Motifs and Sources in the Writings of H. P. Lovecraft." *Lovecraft Annual* No. 2 (2008): 3–87.

Long, Frank Belknap. *Howard Phillips Lovecraft: Dreamer on the Nightside.* Sauk City, WI: Arkham House, 1975.

Lovecraft, H. P. *The Ancient Track: The Complete Poetical Works of H. P. Lovecraft.* Ed. S. T. Joshi. New York: Hippocampus Press, 2013. Revised edition

————. *The Annotated Supernatural Horror in Literature.* Ed. S. T. Joshi. New York: Hippocampus Press, 2000 (rev. ed. 2012).

————. *Collected Essays.* Ed. S. T. Joshi. New York: Hippocampus Press, 2004–06. 5 vols.

————. *Commonplace Book.* Ed. David E. Schultz. West Warwick, RI: Necronomicon Press, 1987.

————. *The Conservative: Complete 1915–1923.* Ed. Marc A. Michaud. West Warwick, RI: Necronomicon Press, 1977.

————. *The Dunwich Horror and Others.* Ed. August Derleth and S. T. Joshi. Sauk City, WI: Arkham House, 1984.

————. *First Writings: Pawtuxet Valley Gleaner, 1906.* Ed. Marc A. Michaud. West Warwick, RI: Necronomicon Press, 1976.

————. *Letters to Robert Bloch.* Ed. David E. Schultz and S. T. Joshi. West Warwick, RI: Necronomicon Press, 1993.

————. "Letters to Carl Ferdinand Strauch." Ed. S. T. Joshi and David E. Schultz. *Lovecraft Annual* No. 4 (2010): 46–119.

————. "Letter to Myrta Alice Little." *Lovecraft Studies* No. 26 (Spring 1992): 26–30.

————. *Letters from New York.* Ed. S. T. Joshi and David E. Schultz. San Francisco: Night Shade Books, 2005.

————. *Letters to Alfred Galpin.* Ed. S. T. Joshi and David E. Schultz. New York: Hippocampus Press, 2003.

————. *Letters to Henry Kuttner.* Ed. David E. Schultz and S. T. Joshi. West Warwick, RI: Necronomicon Press, 1990.

————. *Letters to James F. Morton.* Ed. David E. Schultz and S. T. Joshi. New York: Hippocampus Press, 2011.

————. *Letters to Rheinhart Kleiner.* Ed. David E. Schultz and S. T. Joshi. New York: Hippocampus Press, 2005.

————. *Letters to Samuel Loveman and Vincent Starrett.* Ed. S. T. Joshi and David E. Schultz. West Warwick, RI: Necronomicon Press, 1994.

————. *Miscellaneous Writings.* Ed. S. T. Joshi. Sauk City, WI: Arkham House, 1995.

————. *O Fortunate Floridian: H. P. Lovecraft's Letters to R. H. Barlow.* Ed. S. T. Joshi and David E. Schultz. Tampa, FL: University of Tampa Press, 2007.

————. *The Outsider and Others.* Ed. August Derleth and Donald Wandrei. Sauk City, WI: Arkham House, 1939.

————. *Selected Letters.* Ed. August Derleth, Donald Wandrei, and James Turner. Sauk City, WI: Arkham House, 1965–76. 5 vols.

————. *The Shadow out of Time.* Ed. S. T. Joshi and David E. Schultz. New York: Hippocampus Press, 2001.

————. *The Shadow over Innsmouth.* Ed. S. T. Joshi and David E. Schultz. West Warwick, RI: Necronomicon Press, 1994 (rev. ed. 1997).

————. *To Quebec and the Stars.* Ed. L. Sprague de Camp. West Kingston, RI: Donald M. Grant, 1976.

————. *Writings in the* Tryout. Ed. Marc A. Michaud. West Warwick, RI: Necronomicon Press, 1977.

Lovecraft, H. P., and Willis Conover. *Lovecraft at Last.* Arlington, VA: Carrollton, Clark, 1975.

Lovecraft, H. P., and August Derleth. *Essential Solitude: The Letters of H. P. Lovecraft and August Derleth.* Ed. David E. Schultz and S. T. Joshi. New York: Hippocampus Press, 2008. 2 vols.

Lovecraft, H. P., and Divers Hands. *The Dark Brotherhood and Other Pieces.* Ed. August Derleth. Sauk City, WI: Arkham House, 1966.

Lovecraft, H. P., and Robert E. Howard. *A Means to Freedom: The Letters of H. P. Lovecraft and Robert E. Howard.* Ed. S. T. Joshi, David E. Schultz, and Rusty Burke. New York: Hippocampus Press, 2010. 2 vols.

Lovecraft, H. P., and Fritz Leiber. *Fritz Leiber and H. P. Lovecraft: Writers of the Dark.* Ed. Ben J. S. Szumskyj and S. T. Joshi. Holicong, PA: Wildside Press; 2003.

Lovecraft, H. P., and Donald Wandrei. *Mysteries of Time and Spirit: The Letters of H. P. Lovecraft and Donald Wandrei.* Ed. S. T. Joshi and David E. Schultz. San Francisco: Night Shade Books, 2002.

Marquand, John P. *Lord Timothy Dexter of Newburyport, Massachusetts, First in the East, First in the West, and the Greatest Philosopher in the Western World.* New York: Milton, Balch & Co., 1925.

Munn, H. Warner. "H.P.L.: A Reminiscence." In *Lovecraft Remembered,* ed. Peter Cannon. Sauk City, WI: Arkham House, 1998.

————. *Merlin's Ring.* New York: Ballantine Books, 1974.

Portors, Frank. "Problem for Archaeologists." *Haverhill Evening Gazette* (15 August 1934): 1, 5.

Rothovius, Andrew E. "More on the Great Stone Mysteries." *Yankee* 28 (May 1964): 82–83, 164–171.

Salmonson, Jessica Amanda. "A Dialogue Between *Weird Tales* Author H. Warner Munn & Jessica Amanda Salmonson." Violet Books, accessed July 24, 2012, http://www.violetbooks.com/Munn.html.

"The Shadow out of Time." *BiblioFile: Newsletter of the Brown University Library* 24 (Spring 1995), accessed November 22, 2012, http://www.brown.edu/Facilities/University_Library/publications/Bibliofile/Biblio24/time.html.

Shreffler, Philip A. *The H. P. Lovecraft Companion.* Westport, CT: Greenwood Press, 1977.

Smith, Charles W. "'Tryout' Smith's Autobiography." *Boys' Herald* 72, No. 1 (January 1943): 2–4.

Smith, Clark Ashton. *Letters to H. P. Lovecraft.* Ed. Steve Behrends. West Warwick, RI: Necronomicon Press, 1987.

Spencer, Truman J. *The History of Amateur Journalism.* New York: The Fossils, 1957.

Thoreau, Henry David. *The Writings of Henry David Thoreau.* Boston: Houghton Mifflin, 1906. 20 vols.

Wetzel, George T. *The Lovecraft Scholar.* Darien, CT: Hobgoblin Press, 1983.

Williams, Blanche Colton. *O. Henry Memorial Award Prize Stories of 1932.* Garden City, NY: Doubleday, Doran, 1932.

INDEX

189

CPSIA information can be obtained at www.ICGtesting.com
Printed in the USA
LVOW01s1317100913

351817LV00006B/71/P